KONRAD BARTELSKI

THE AUTOBIOGRAPHY OF A SKIER

KONRAD BARTELSKI

THE AUTOBIOGRAPHY OF A SKIER

KONRAD BARTELSKI
——WITH——
MALCOLM SEVERS

WILLOW BOOKS
Collins
8 Grafton Street, London
1983

Willow Books
William Collins Sons & Co Ltd
London · Glasgow · Sydney · Auckland · Toronto · Johannesburg

First published in Great Britain 1983

Bartelski, Konrad
Konrad Bartelski
1. Bartelski, Konrad 2. Skis and skiing
Great Britain—Biography
I. Title
796.93′092′4   GV854.2.B

ISBN 0 00 218041 3

Filmset in Times by Ace Filmsetting Ltd, Frome, Somerset
Printed and bound in Great Britain by
Wm Collins Sons & Co Ltd, Glasgow

CONTENTS

To Peter

FOREWORD

Individuals of note pass through the skiing world only on rare occasions. Most of us are familiar with the names of Killy, Moser-Proell and Klammer. But such renown is not always limited to those who have excelled – there is also a place for those who have contributed to the sport in time, dedication, and thought, individuals who have made skiing a better sport than it was when they arrived on the scene.

Konrad Bartelski is one of those few. I have had the pleasure of being associated with Konrad throughout his World Cup career, and have seen for myself his contribution to skiing: a contribution which has not been limited to the British sport, but which has had a profound influence at international level too.

Konrad brought character to the World Cup tour. He showed dogged determination in carrying the colours of Britain, often in the face of adversity, but finally achieved success – a dream realised which had been held since his early days, training in the Scottish Highlands with Willy Bailey and the late Peter Fuchs. Although victory eluded Konrad in the end, his results in the 1981–82 season meant much more to me than a second place finish in the World Cup downhill at Val Gardena, Italy. He became – literally – the only 'outsider' (not an Austrian, Swiss or Canadian) in the top seed; he showed us all that spirit and experience are such valuable tools for competition. He demonstrated, too, that even non-alpine country skiers can aspire to the peaks of international ski racing. Yet still he had time to look beyond ski competition into the inner workings of the sport, and to comment on how he saw that it could be made better – for us all.

KEN READ
11 May 1983

— 1 —
THE WEEK OF
SUCCESS

Coming on to the final straight there was just one critical jump to the finish. Every muscle screamed with the effort and a head cold that had dogged me all week had set my eyes streaming and my head throbbing; concentration was impossible. In previous years I had never had any problems at the last jump but this time, of all times, my watering eyes forced me to tuck my head into my body just a little too much. The result was that when the bump arrived I was out of synch – I mistimed it and the impetus shot me into the air. Inside I was screaming to myself 'keep straight . . . keep straight . . . keep standing up', but the error had forced me onto the back of my skis. For all of those few, but tormentingly long, yards to the finish, I was struggling for control.

Once through the finish gate I knew I had skied well, and I didn't know how I could possibly have skied any faster. But, good run or not, I hardly dared look at the time clock – a bad result at Val d'Isère the week before had hit me hard and I couldn't bear the prospect of such a depression again. Suddenly I became aware of a buzz of excitement in the crowd and my hopes began to rise. The thought that just possibly I might have made the top twenty began to edge out the gloom of imagined failure. Now I had to look at the clock . . . 2.07. My reaction was immediate: I didn't know what my actual position was, but I knew I was fast and amongst the leaders. I couldn't contain my elation.

The unbounded joy that I experienced at Val Gardena that December Sunday in 1981 was the complete opposite of the despair caused by a miserable result the week before in Val d'Isère. There I had to rummage through the results sheets to find my name stuck on the third page in sixty-first place. It was my worst result for longer than I cared to remember and the worst possible way to start the new season.

Somehow, though, I felt cheated. I had not skied badly, certainly not badly enough to be six seconds behind the leaders, but we had been having trouble with our skis all week and, despite all our efforts, just could not get them to run well. I had been slow in the practice and, although not six seconds slower than the quick men, it was obvious that the skis were not up to scratch. Indeed, they were running so badly that I could not possibly see how they could be made competitive for the races to come. It was frustrating and depressing, and failure dominated my thinking. Even a party thrown by Ken Read, who had come back from an injury to a triumphant fifth place, could not shake my mood. Ken's placing had won him a small mountain of cheese from the Salomon competition chief who had bet that Ken wouldn't make it into the first ten. Obviously the only way for Ken to celebrate his good fortune was to throw a party. Invitations went out to Steve Podborski, Laurie Graham, Gerry Sorenson, myself and a few others and the *Beaujolais Nouveau* corks began to pop. But, try as I might, and I did try, I could not raise my spirits. After a while I slipped out and tagged along rather aimlessly with Canadian 'B' team member Robin McLeish and a few of his friends. Like a magnet drawing pins we were pulled into a bar, but the conviviality only deepened my depression.

Even so, I had been racing long enough to know that races in the past are dead races . . . the only ones that count are the ones to come. Deeply entrenched defence mechanisms began to take over and I knew that the only way out was to prepare my campaign strategy for the next race at Val Gardena. Despite the clouds in my head I started to build the structure of this next assault. Thoughts of travelling, ski testing, training, all flashed through my mind and, as they passed, stubborn resolve began to erode the gloom. By the time I went to bed the seeds of hope had been sown and I was determined to approach the week with optimism, however cautious.

When morning came there was no time for thinking of any sort. I had to herd up the rest of the British team – a motley crew comprising myself, Stuart Fitzsimmons, Freddie Burton and Ronald Duncan (alias Boris) – and load them into our well-used Tricentrol Ford Transit van for the long haul through the Mont Blanc tunnel to Val Gardena. Even in high spirits this journey, which we had all done many times before, was trying, to say the least. The van was crowded with skis, bags and bodies. The suspension transmitted every bump in the road to our spines and the vibration and noise from the engine set ears tingling and nerves on edge. Light relief came only from Stuart's collection of cassettes. If it hadn't been for the music of Dire Straits, the boredom of that twisty road would have compounded the race-day doldrums of the previous day.

Once through the Mont Blanc tunnel, the interminable twists and turns gave way to the monotony of the motorway. Fortunately it was sunny and Stuart was in a playful mood; so much so that a little of his good humour brushed off onto me. I was glad that we were travelling in the van as, once in the seat of a comfortable car, Stuart had a habit of falling immediately into a foetal position and plummetting into sleep. Our van's convincing imitation of a pneumatic drill effectively put paid to this normal and unsociable routine, so I was entertained by his cheerful banter all the way into Italy. One particularly delightful moment was a conversation Stuart had through the mouth of his latest toy – a furry, clockwork St Bernard dog. Upon seeing a real, doe-eyed St Bernard sitting in the back of a Range Rover we were following, Stuart put his onto the dash and proceeded to arouse the interest of the larger version in front. The words and jokes of the incident are, of course, long gone from my mind but I do remember the tonic of the laughter, and for that I will always be grateful to Stuart the clown: he was our court jester.

Eight o'clock in the evening saw us into Val Gardena, where I began unpacking the van with mixed feelings. This unforgiving downhill course had been the scene of some of my best and worst performances and I couldn't help wondering what the fickle mountain had in store for me now. Again I was stopped from wallowing in morbid thoughts – this time by the wonderful Giorgi family who run the Hotel Laurin. On other visits their cheerfulness and wonderful food had made the hotel a longed-for home from home. They treated us with real affection. On this occasion they interrupted the unloading of the van to insist we devour plates of steaming and delicious pasta. Of all the memories of that week – and they are legion – that pasta comes somewhere near the top. It cheered me up considerably.

Another cheering aspect about the hotel was that for the first time

I had my own ski technician staying under the same roof. Ernst Habesatter, an Atomic ski technician who looked after the American team, had been assigned by Atomic to look after my skis as well. I was hopeful that this closer relationship would lead to more productive testing of the skis through the training sessions.

At breakfast the following morning our trainer, Koni Rupprechter, ran through the programme for the first training day. There was to be an inspection of the course at ten o'clock and the first timed training run at noon. I collected the skis that Ernst had selected for me to try that day, and rode the lift for the slow and important inspection.

At the top all the teams gathered with their trainers and, at ten precisely, were marshalled on to the course by the officials. At this time the trainers and the racers check the course for racing line, bumps, changes in terrain, snow conditions, preparation of the course and landmarks that can be used to set bearings and time the start of turns. It is a painstaking and thorough appraisal.

When inspecting the course it is not so much skied as sideslipped. Every little factor and nuance must be noted for incorporation into the final run plan. Each turn, bump, rut and gradient must be so clear in the racer's mind that it is anticipated; none must ever come as a surprise. Koni and I noticed that the top of the run was pretty much the same as in previous years, but we were glad to see that some of the more vicious bumps had become slightly more rounded than usual meaning that they would give less of a kick and less time in the air – a condition that suited my style of skiing.

Lower down the course runs into a section of forest with some icy and tricky 'S' bends. We both spent a good deal of time on this section as I felt it was the key to success or failure. If I could get up sufficient speed here it would stay with me for the rest of the run and I was sure I could put in a good time.

Out of the forest the Val Gardena course runs into that section known throughout the world as the Camel Bumps. Skiing the flat section that leads to these bumps, although seemingly innocuous to an observer, is a little like heading towards the edge of the white cliffs of Dover. All the skier can see is the mountains of the opposite side of the valley, with a white slope horizon-line halfway up that hides a sheer drop into two very nasty and jolting bumps. Taking these bumps fast is difficult, because there is a tendency to be thrown off balance into the third bump before there has been time to complete the second properly. It is a bit like being on a bucking bronco. If you get it right, however, the sensation is more like that of a flat stone skimming over a pond.

When we reached the Camel Bumps we noticed that all the teams had gathered and seemed to be engaged in heated discussion. The Austrian coach, Karl Kahr, and the Swiss coach, Karl Fresner, were arguing bitterly about the location of the control flag for the second hump. The Austrian was keen to retain the old location because in the 1980 race Uli Spiess had used the line to jump off the second bump, completely clearing the third before landing – the first time that this had been done. Quite obviously Kahr was hoping Spiess could do the same again and gain an advantage for Austria. Fresner, on the other hand, had more respect for the sanity of racers and was pushing for a modification to the course that would dictate a safer and more sensible line. Fortunately sanity won this battle. To give a racer the opportunity to gain time by jumping 150 feet at 80mph would have been ridiculous. In order to win everyone would have had to try it and, inevitably, there would have been casualties. By letting common sense have sway the organisers created conditions likely to allow the racers to enjoy a happy Christmas.

Once the modification was finally established, it was decided to have another inspection from the halfway mark to let the skiers become conversant with the new line. Koni and I checked it very carefully and then slipped down to the Czaslat corners, entry to which would be crucial if I was going to be able to pick up time on other racers.

Skiing these turns is like skiing on corrugated boiler plate. They make your leg muscles pump like shock absorbers on a bumpy car testing track, yet they require great precision if you are to get the most out of the undulating terrain.

Once I had logged the bumps and possible pitfalls in my memory, I skied the long right-hander into the finishing straight and checked out the last bump on the course – an innocuous-looking mound about fifty metres from the finish gate. This bump had presented few problems to me in the past but I knew it could be tricky as many top racers had been caught out by it. I was anxious to discover any hidden terrors it might hold this time, but there seemed to be none.

With my head bursting with the information gathered from the inspection and my mind's eye working overtime, going over and over the course, I headed back to the top for the first of the all-important practices.

At the restaurant by the start the teams were huddled in groups for last-minute preparations. The more introverted racers stood apart, deep in their private thoughts, while the extroverts cracked jokes together. All ski racers have their own way, whether by meditation or by joking, of meeting the pressures that build up before a race. This of course was not a race, only a practice, but the same pressures existed and each skier had to cope with them in his own particular way. No matter what the personality type of the individual racer, most had the comfort of a team for succour. The Swiss stood out as a group in their white suits, as did the Canadians in their yellow. Even the Russians, who sat quietly in a corner, were noticeably a team – a group from which each individual could draw strength. In Freddie Burton and Boris I had a team too, but I was not drawn to them. Instead I headed for the people I most wanted to be with – my friends on the Canadian and Norwegian teams. These were the people I could relate to, discuss the course with and verify my own feelings about the way the course would run. It was unfortunate, but true, that Freddie and Boris simply could not supply the level of team back-up that I needed.

Eventually the racers began to drift out for their runs. The usual routine is to go out early for a quick warm-up before the run itself. This loosens muscles and helps to neutralise the pressure. Some argue that as these runs are practice they lack the stress and agony of a race. That is rubbish. Practices are not only for getting to know the course, but also for testing skis. Unless the skis are skied fast it is impossible for the technicians to judge how they will run in a race so the onus is on the racer to ski just as hard as he would if the World Cup depended on it.

As the first runners went off, most of the others, including myself, watched from the top to see how they performed. It is always something of a boost to do this as the inspection run sometimes has the effect of making things a little larger than life. The apparent ease with which the early runners handle the course helps to bring it into perspective: to reduce it from the superhuman to something that fit and skilled ordinary humans can conceivably accomplish. It has always amazed me how a run that seems daunting on first inspection becomes manageable when you are actually out there skiing it. The efforts of the early runners are thus psychologically important. If they are skiing fluently and fast you know you can too, and if they are making mistakes you see where these are happening and are able to amend your own run plan to suit.

But before you know it your turn has come and, at start number 31, mine came. I took the skis Ernst had selected, code numbered 111 for identification, and had a last-minute talk with Koni on the radio to see how the course was looking from his position at the bottom. The track didn't seem to be exhibiting any particular problems and the new route over the Camel Bumps was going as smoothly as planned so I started that training run with more confidence than I would have believed possible when I left Val d'Isère.

The first run on any course is always exciting. No matter how well you know the mountain from previous years it always seems able to throw up some new challenge that effectively puts it into the realm of the unknown. Each course has its own character and the first run is like an introduction. It is an almost eerie experience as the mountain exposes its new self – yet you know you must come to terms with it quickly as, whether you like the new character or not, this is your place of work for the next few days and your ability or inability to master it will be reflected when the men are finally sorted from the boys on race day. The excitement of the Val Gardena course comes from its speed and its long, fast turns. It demands good technique but has a rhythm and fluidity that make it – if you get it right, that is – one of the most satisfying of all the World Cup courses. Certainly when you pull up in the Val Gardena finish area there is always exhilaration, a feeling of accomplishment, irrespective of the time on the clock.

This was as true for me as it had always been. The course had been prepared well (which when you are starting at number 31 is critical), the new line through the Camel Bumps meant your teeth stayed in your mouth instead of shooting up to the top of your head, and the entry to Czaslat required precision but was slick and fast.

Despite all this, however, I was over five seconds down on the fastest time. It was disappointing but, at this stage anyway, not the end of the world. There were still two days of training to go and I had never been the kind of skier who could produce a full, race-day head of steam in practice.

Later, discussing the session with Koni, we realised that I had taken a poor line into Czaslat. This had slowed me down through the 'esses' and, once lost, that speed is virtually impossible to pick up on the final sections.

We decided to concentrate our efforts on Czaslat in the practices to come but, before any final decisions could be taken on changes to the line, I had to see the video and compare my section times with those of other racers. Of the two the video, for me, was the most important – it was something I had come to rely on as a pointer to faster times. Important though it was, however, watching the video could be something of a chore. Sitting in a bleak room watching racer after racer flash by can have a hypnotising effect, lulling the viewer into a sort of trance from which it is very difficult to read the information the film has to offer. On this occasion our films had been taken by Stuart Fitzsimmons, who is unable to do anything without injecting a touch of the comic. Stuart was only in his early apprenticeship as a video cameraman but he had flair. As well as filming all the important racers at all the important turns and bumps, he had also devoted some footage to the younger, lesser lights. Watching the faces of some of these youngsters as they registered anxiety and apprehension on the more difficult parts of the course was a tonic for me. I was able to laugh a little and, although the serious purpose of the viewing was never forgotten, managed to get some good, relaxing enjoyment out of this normally tedious job. The entertainment value of the viewing session was further enhanced by the addition of Stuart's Sony Walkman cassette deck into the system – the music making even the mundane sequences enjoyable.

For me, however, there were few of those. I could learn something from most of the racers and I had to pick out what I was doing wrong in comparison with the others.

Of particular interest was the run of Franz Klammer. Franz had always been very strong on the Czaslat section and, sure enough, he clocked the fastest time. Watching him, his skis seemed to fly over the course and his line appeared to be the best of the day. He was skiing with great confidence following his remarkable victory in Val d'Isère and there seemed to be no stopping him. Even so I felt it was possible to improve on Franz's line and I resolved to experiment with two alternative lines at the next day's practice.

In the video room I started to be aware of the first niggling signs of a cold so I went to see the doctor who travels with the American team for some pills and nose drops. At that stage I wasn't too worried about it – it was just minor sniffles and there was little discomfort. Unfortunately it was not to stay that way.

While in the American camp I picked up a copy of the section times that the race organisers had compiled. These revealed that I was losing too much time at the top of the course; not very encouraging. But there was worse to come. On independent times that the Americans had taken on the flat, gliding section of the course, I was a full second slower on a 15-second timed segment. This was a disaster. In ski racing, one second out of 15 is an eternity. I was very, very low indeed when I showed these times to Ernst, my technician. Like all technicians he was taciturn at the news and responded simply by saying that he would prepare two other pairs of skis for the next practice – which he started to do straight away. Seeing him then I knew I was lucky to have Ernst in my camp. Although almost painfully introverted, he was thoroughly dedicated to his craft. A really good ski technician is worth his weight in gold in the downhill racing game: and Ernst was one of the very best.

However, although I knew he was good and that he would do all he could to help me win races, I felt the need to give him a little extra incentive: he stood to gain a bottle of champagne for every World Cup point I picked up in the season! It was a light-hearted gesture, but one that was to have its happy side for both of us within just a few days.

That evening after dinner I tried to relax over a coffee with Stuart before going to the bar in the hope of bumping into some English chalet girls. Despite the beginnings of the cold, I was not one to let the possibility of a little English female company go begging. It is always nice if there is a chalet girl or two around, as I find their talk of bizarre chalet guests, cooking, and news from home, a welcome relief from the pressures and anxieties that are never far from the surface when racers talk amongst themselves. But this time I was out of luck, so I was in bed early to be as fresh as possible for the Thursday practice.

Unfortunately I was no better in the two Thursday practices than I had been in Wednesday's. I skied the steeper bits of the course quite well but my times on the flats were still very slow. Even though I knew in my mind that the answer lay in the skis it was impossible not to start thinking that perhaps the fault was in me. Certainly doubts about my own ability to ski the course fast began to creep in and, with my head cold deepening, I was not the jolliest person when the day's practice was over. On the video playback I noticed that I was skiing some parts of the course better than anyone else, but when I looked at the overall times I was not even in the hunt. It was with growing despair that I asked myself 'what is it that I have to do?' . . . 'what can I do?' Try as I might, though, I could not see a way out.

The miseries were dissipated with dinner. Normally in the last few days before a race my habit was to eat alone or with the other English boys, but on this particular night I found myself eating with Ken Read and the Austrians, Uli Spiess and Harti Weirather.

The four of us had been friends for some time, we got on well together and the table conversation was charged with good humour. Our amusement was heightened by the presence on the other side of the room of World Cup ski 'mafia' boss Serge Lang, who was eyeing us suspiciously. He knew that we were all serious about our sport and he knew that we all had definite ideas about the way the sport should go in the future. For him the sight of skiers from three countries eating together two days before a major race could only mean trouble. We enjoyed his discomfort.

Friday, the last day of practice, was the final chance I had to raise my flagging enthusiasm and get things together on the slope. My cold was getting progressively worse but the weather could not have been better: if I was going to make it, it had to be today. But when I saw my time at the bottom – 4.76 seconds slower than the leader – I was all set to pack my bags and head for home. In ski racing, when you are 4.76 seconds behind, you are not just behind the leader you are behind everyone. It is like being 4.76 laps behind the winner in a Grand Prix. It was an unmitigated disaster and the prospect of a full season of similar failures started me wondering whether the whole shooting match was worth the trouble. I was as disillusioned as I had ever been in my career.

On race day my cold was at its height. My head was heavy and my nose blocked; the last thing I wanted to do was race. But a race day was a race day and there was a routine to follow. First thing was to check the weather – it wasn't too bad. At least it was a whole lot better than I felt. As usual the race-day mechanism took over and I switched myself off from the things around me to concentrate solely on the two minutes of race to come. I did my exercises and had my obligatory jog. I don't enjoy these things even on good days, but this day even my anticipation was gone – I was drained.

Nevertheless the race-day routine had to continue, and the next step was to see what was happening in the ski-room. Ernst, without any hesitation and with his usual emotionless, almost brusque, manner pointed at the 111 skis. With a similar lack of emotion I accepted them. These were the skis that had done nothing for me on the first practice day but none of the skis had been exactly brilliant and it was six of one and half a dozen of the other. I accepted Ernst's decision despite the fact that my normal race-day habit was to choose the skis myself in consultation with Koni. For this race the choice was between eight pairs of bad runners: I had to take Ernst's selection and hope for the best. Anyway, all I wanted to do was to get the day over as quickly as possible, it didn't matter what I used.

As the previous day had been too warm to hold an inspection without damaging the course, the organisers decided to hold one before the race. I warmed up with some free skiing before going over to the start for a final look at the hill. In the start hut itself a young French racer, Guy Pessey, approached me and said, 'Hey, have you heard, the Russians have moved into Poland.' I was stunned. My father had family in Poland and he had always feared that if the Russians moved in his family would be in trouble. For me it was the last nail in the coffin. On the inspection I hardly saw the course – all I could see were images of the Russian racers hanging from the trees. At the bottom I tried to get more details about the situation in Poland but all I could do was confirm that what Guy had told me was correct. I could hardly think through my cold and now my father's country had been invaded – just a few minutes before a major race.

On the way back to the start I had nothing more in my mind than to get the race run and the day over and done with. I wanted to get back on the road and on to a new place where I could start afresh.

In the restaurant near the start I tried to sit apart and concentrate but it was a waste of time – I was just wallowing in my own misery. I needed to talk to someone so I joined a Norwegian racer, Even Hole, and Thor, his trainer. Rather in the way of the confessional I poured out my troubles but, despite their kindness and concern, I was not able to lift my mood or develop the tense excitement necessary if you are to do well in a race. A good cup of tea and an English face would have been appreciated but Stuart Fitzsimmons, who probably would not have had any money on him anyway, was at the start taking pictures of the stars.

Alone, and feeling it sorely, I changed into my racing suit and donned my start number: 29. As I put the number on I recalled, for some reason that I still do not understand, a piece of advice given to me the previous September by Phil Fearon, a sports psychologist at St Mary's, Twickenham. Phil had told me that in high-speed sports the body reacts to what it has been trained to do on instinct. He said that if the mind was thinking too much it got in the way of the instinct process and performance was impaired. During a quick radio call to Koni for last-minute course conditions and the times of the early runners, this advice lingered in my mind.

Once in the starting gate I knew that the fastest time was 2.07 and something, but I didn't care. With my mind completely empty I exploded through the starting wand and into the blazing sunshine that washed the course.

From the start I had no thought of winning. I was, however, anxious to avoid giving the impression that I wasn't trying so I got my head down into a good position and hoped it would at least look as though I had my mind on the job. My only concern was getting the race over without looking a twit.

I remember very little of the top part of the course through the flats but the jump into the forest carried me wide because of ruts and I landed a bit off line – that woke me up a bit. The bad, at least I thought it was bad, line meant that I had to delay my entry into Czaslat by a metre. It made me concentrate. At the time I had no idea that the press, the spectators and the other racers were all

concentrating on Czaslat too. Their interest was caused by amazement. I had the fastest time at the first split-time – nobody could
believe that I would still be fastest at the second. At the bottom Erwin
Resch was being congratulated live by Austrian television. He had a
solid lead and the best guys were already down. Everyone thought it
was all over bar the shouting but when the split-time for Czaslat
came up and I was still fastest people began to look up. They could
all see the possibility of a major upset – everybody, that is, but me.

I was hardly bothered with the turns but I landed on the line I
wanted so I thought only of keeping my weight on the downhill ski
and my shoulders low. On the final bend, however, I was beginning
to feel the effects of my cold and the strength was ebbing from my
legs. My head felt as though it was rolling about on my shoulders
but, even though my eyes were streaming, I desperately tried to give
all my attention to that last jump. The botch that I made of it seemed
minor at the time – I didn't know that that one small error had cost
me the race. The only thought in my mind was relief that it was all
over. Little did I realise that the day had only really begun.

There it was . . . 2:07.53. It was fantastic. With that time I knew I
had to be in the top ten. It wasn't until Luigi, a friend from the village
who had been looking after my jacket at the bottom, yelled 'second'
that I began to realise what all the excitement was about. I almost
forgot to take my skis off for the customary PR pose for television.

Peter Müller was the first racer to grab me and hug me in con-
gratulation. He was very happy for me but said, 'If only you hadn't
opened up at the bottom'. I didn't know what he meant. I had no
idea I was actually breathing down the neck of the winner. When the
dust finally settled I managed to get the full picture. Eleven-hun-
dredths of a second separated me from Irwin Resch. I was second,
ahead of Olympic gold medal winner Leonard Stock, with Steve
Podborski pushed back into fourth place.

Only then did the reality of it hit me. Things started to happen in
a blur. Interviews in Italian, French, German – all at the same time.
Typically, it was Austrian journalists who asked me if I thought my
good time was caused by the course speeding up for the later
runners. The question really annoyed me. It wasn't as though we
had been skiing on a new snow course (which might have helped
the higher start numbers) and none of the racers just in front of me

had any spectacular times to show. I was sure that if it had been an Austrian who had recorded my time there would have been no suggestion of help from the course.

Many of the other racers, shocked by the result and hardly believing it, rushed off to see the video. They didn't know that I was more shocked than any of them. I was happy, of course, but in some ways I was also disappointed. I had worked for ten years trying for this success, believing that, when it came, it would be through some supreme effort; something extra-special. The disappointment was that it was all so simple. I couldn't understand why it had taken me so long.

But these disappointments could not hide my elation. There I was, in the finish area of a major World Cup downhill, having achieved what I had set out to do. The Union Jack was flying proudly above the winners' rostrum for the first time ever. Life for me was now completely changed. I knew that winning was possible.

— 2 —
ACQUIRING SKI-LEGS

With an uncharacteristic disregard for the convenience of my mother, I decided to come into this world at 3.40 on the morning of 27 May, 1954: a Gemini. My father, Jan, had managed by the skin of his teeth to get out of Poland at the beginning of the war. He had had the Russians at his back and the Germans in front but was still able to make his way to England where he joined the RAF as a flyer. Throughout the war he flew Wellington anti-submarine aircraft for Coastal Command and, when the war ended in 1945, was determined to continue his flying in civilian life. He was unable to get a job with the British airlines as there were thousands of former service flyers after only a few jobs but he was successful in landing a job with the Dutch airline, KLM, in Amsterdam. It was there that I was born.

In Poland my father had not been particularly interested in winter sports or mountains but, as part of his flight training in 1942, found himself in Medicine Hat, Alberta: a Canadian Air Force training centre near Calgary. This, of course, was prime ski country. It was near the Rockies of the British Columbia/Alberta border and the resort settlement of Banff. My father used his leisure time to sightsee in the mountains and, although he didn't actually ski at this time, developed a strong desire to do so should it be possible when the war was over. During this time he saw Lake Louise, and it is ironic that forty-one years later the wheel should turn full circle. Lake Louise was the venue for my final race and the actual decision to retire was made there. When I rang my father to tell him what I had decided all he could say was 'How is the Lake – is it still as beautiful as I remember it?' It was like a circle of life being completed: I had closed the circle begun by my father. It seemed appropriate that I should end this phase of my life here and begin anew. Who knows, maybe a son of mine will someday complete the cycle I am just beginning now.

Immediately after the war my father found a job flying charter aircraft between Blackpool and the Isle of Man and it was at this time that he met and married Pamela Vickers, the daughter of a Blackpool civil engineer. With this extra responsibility he took British nationality and tried hard to land a more secure job with BOAC. It was only when he realised that the chances of such a job were remote that he took the position with KLM.

But once settled into Amsterdam life my father was able to fulfil his wartime desire to learn to ski. He began to take an annual week's holiday in the Austrian resort of Kitzbühel and there I, as a tottering three-year-old, first felt skis under my feet.

For someone who was to go on and ski in World Cup downhills it was not an auspicious start. Not only did I find it difficult to stand up, I didn't care much for the snow and the cold. Indeed, I preferred to spend most of my time in the lavatory – not because of too much Coca-Cola, but because it was the warmest place on the hill. One of my earliest memories is of being locked in with my father hammering on the door to get me out.

At three I was considered too young for the ski school, and those first faltering steps and tumbles were taken from the safety of between my father's legs. But safe though it was I wasn't happy there. I couldn't understand why I wasn't allowed to join the ski school. I saw my brother Stefan, three years older than me, having fun with the other boys. I wanted to be with them too and this spurred me on. It has occurred to me on many occasions since that without Stefan to emulate my life might well have taken a very different turn.

Over the next seven years we went to Kitzbühel as a family every January for six days. On the first day we were given a blue ticket and I soon learned that skiing was best when the ticket was full and was miserable when there was only one clip, representing the last day of the holiday, left to be punched. Each year as I got to love skiing more and more so the sadness I felt on the last day increased. But I did, eventually, get into the ski school and I started to take a pride in my progress. Of course six days a year is not very long and the progress was slow, but my father was keen to help and on the last day would take movies for us to watch when we got back to Amsterdam. Those home movies kept me going all through the summer. I watched them and learned from them and dreamed about being better: I wanted nothing more than to be a good skier. The year between holidays seemed interminably long.

One of my most vivid memories from those days as a small boy skiing in Kitzbühel came when I was big enough to peer over a fence to watch the racers flashing by. The crowds that gathered by the fence would cheer when the faster local men went past but the cheers would turn to laughter when it was the turn of the British competitors. The British racers were always the slowest and the locals would quite openly jeer at them. They considered that the British boys had no chance; that they were amateurs who skied for fun, with no possibility of ever being anything but last.

I could never understand this. From my earliest days I felt that if a British skier trained hard and had the right attitude he would be able to beat the Austrians and the Swiss at their own game. It seemed to me inconceivable that the people who lived in the Alps should be faster than anyone else just because of where they lived. I was convinced, as I was to be throughout my career, that, once the proper technique had been mastered, the only difference between racers was in the degree of their desire to get to the bottom of the hill first. The man with the strongest desire could just as easily be British as anything else. Because I felt this to be so it hurt when I heard the laughter at the puny and ineffective efforts of the British kids. I became determined to show one day that the British could be just as competitive on the slopes as anyone else.

What I needed was a good instructor, one with the flair to drive me on and the technique to perfect my own embryonic style. In my fifth year of skiing, as a precocious eight-year-old, I found her.

Gitti Schatz, at sixteen, was the prettiest ski instructor in the school; she also taught the top class. At the time I was in the second-to-top class and, more than anything, I wanted to be in hers. That winter I devoted all my energies to getting promoted: not so much because I wanted to be taught by her but because I wanted to be skiing with the prettiest girl.

As it turned out, Gitti was not only the prettiest but she was also the best. Even as a teenager she was regarded as a shining star in the ski school. She had a faultless technique (a technique that was eventually to see her travelling the world demonstrating the Austrian style of skiing) and an easy way of teaching. She taught me that the best way of improving was to be constantly in control. Instead of introducing me to racing she showed me the back of beyond of the Kitzbühel mountains. Together we skied the untracked powder slopes and I learned the importance of applied technique and control if I was to be able to cope with the rapidly changing conditions of ice, wind crust and soft snow that we encountered on most of the runs. With her help I won my Kitzbühel Gold Book which was awarded for skiing twenty different named runs in the area. It was my first trophy – and the pride I felt then was comparable to anything I have felt since. Gitti built the solid foundations that my skiing needed and she cultivated and directed my growing confidence. My admiration and respect for her knew no bounds. What she said was gospel, and I trusted her implicitly. I could not have had a better start.

Year by year my love of skiing grew and, in 1966, my parents found themselves in a position to take me for two weeks instead of the usual one. At this time my brother and I were attending the English School in the Hague and he was doing his 'O' levels. In order not to take up his school time while we were in Kitzbühel my father decided to send Stefan away to the Dutch Ski Federation's junior race fortnight over the Christmas period. At the end of this fortnight Stefan arrived home thoroughly delighted. He had taken part in the Dutch junior championships and had come tenth in the giant slalom. He had enjoyed it so much that my father decided that I could go on the same fortnight the following year.

After Stefan's first year, however, he stayed at school while I went with my parents for that first glorious fortnight in the snow. As usual I had Gitti as my instructor but this time we found ourselves skiing while the Austrian team were practising on the Hahnenkamm. While we were skiing down, the star of the Austrian team, and my own personal hero, Karl Schranz, saw us and skied over to join us. He knew Gitti well and I thought he was coming just to pass the time of day. But when we had all stopped, he said to her, 'You have a fine young skier there. He will make a good racer.' I could hardly believe my ears. To hear that said from the mouth of Karl Schranz was as much as a young boy could take. Suddenly I began to think about racing seriously for the first time. If Karl Schranz thought I had

26

the makings of a racer there must be something there and, if there was, I was going to find it.

Unfortunately Gitti and I were unable to get down to the nitty-gritty of race training as the words of the great man came almost at the end of that particular holiday. Instead of learning the discipline of the slalom poles I had to return to the discipline of the classroom. However my skiing for that year was not yet over. At Easter my mother took me, along with my brother and grandfather, to Scotland for a week's skiing. I was really excited. The prospect of skiing in my own country was very heady and I looked forward with relish to getting the feel of the Scottish hills. We had planned to stay in the Struan House hotel of the Fuchs family in Carrbridge because Karl Fuchs also ran the Austrian Ski School of the area and we were keen to benefit from their instruction. Unfortunately Struan House was full and we had to find accommodation elsewhere – a misfortune that delayed for four years my meeting with Peter Fuchs, Karl's son, who was to become my best friend and my closest skiing colleague.

While we were there the Scottish Junior Championships were taking place in Cairngorm and I determined there and then that the following year I would take part in the races myself. I was still only eleven but the prospect of taking on the local Scots fired me. I tried to get over to where the races were being held to get some idea of the slopes and the conditions but the weather – surely the worst aspect of skiing in Scotland – stopped me from seeing too much and I had to be content with a resolve to compete without really knowing what I was likely to be up against.

Back in Holland, I had the Belgian and Dutch Grand Prix to look forward to in the summer, but after they had gone by, all I could think about was the winter and the racing to come.

Just before Christmas the great day came. I found myself huddled on Rotterdam station waiting for the train that would take me to the Dutch Ski Federation's training camp. I was twelve, and a short twelve at that, and I was going away to ski by myself for the first time. On the train I found myself amongst dozens of other young people on the same adventure and I discovered that skiing was fun off as well as on the slopes. By luck or design I don't know – after all, I was only twelve! – I found myself in a compartment with some of the prettier girls on the trip. They were about two years older than me but it didn't seem to make any difference and we had a great time – not only with a little teenage canoodling on the bunks but also in keeping out other members of the group who wanted to join in our fun.

Our destination was Neustift, near Innsbruck. The slopes there were a revelation to me, but not as much as the skiing of my companions. They had all had race training before and they skied very fast, much faster than me. My previous training had been devoted to style and technique, whereas they had been weaned on speed: it took a lot for me even to keep up with them in the free skiing. Once I was shown the slalom course, however, it was a different matter. For some reason I revelled in the discipline imposed by the slalom course and I was soon skiing it quite fast – faster in fact than most of the others. Being so short, I was on tiny skis compared with the other racers and some joked that I was only going down fast because I was skiing on tooth-picks; but the races would be the real test.

The first race was the giant slalom. I crashed – so I got the two over in one bang, my first race and my first crash. But it was no ordinary crash. I didn't pile into the snow until ten metres from the end of the course and, slide and scrabble though I did after the fall, I finally stopped with my nose in the snow inches from the line. I was very cross with myself but my brother Stefan was fourth and I knew I had skied quite well until the fall. I knew better performances would come.

One of the problems Stefan and I faced was that we were not Dutch. Because of this the authorities decided that we could not compete as fully accredited competitors but only *hors de concours*. That was my first experience of politics in sport and an early lesson that some administrators can only go by the book – no matter what the individual circumstances. It was some consolation at the end of the fortnight, after Stefan and I had put up some good performances, when the authorities tried to pressure us into getting Dutch passports. We, of course, wanted to stay British, but at the same time it was nice to know that our efforts had been appreciated.

The cause of this flurry to get us into the Dutch squad was the slalom on the final day. On the first run I was leading with Stefan in second place, half a second behind. Then on the second run Stefan found another gear and won, with me second, six-tenths of a second in his wake. That made Stefan the overall winner and me the runner-up, with just a tenth of a second separating us. I didn't know it then but second place was to become the story of my life.

I was pretty pleased with this performance. Little pipsqueak Bartelski, hardly bigger than a shrimp, had triumphed over the Dutch junior racers. It was satisfying, but I knew that the Dutch kids were lowlanders without much of a reputation. I knew too that the British Junior Championships that I had set my sights on would be a much stiffer test.

The biggest problem with the British Championships was financial. We had had our skiing holiday for that year and there was no money left in the kitty. It was out of the question for my father to find the money to fly us to Scotland and put us up in a hotel. Persistent nagging finally persuaded my grandfather to take us up to the Cairngorms in his caravan. This solved the accommodation problem; the next was the actual skiing. Stefan and I had no spare cash for lift passes so our uphill transport was our own feet. Every morning we would trudge up the mountain for training, setting branches and twigs into the snow for slalom poles. Now and again we would look enviously over at the others enjoying the lifts and proper slalom courses but we were there and we were skiing. It was what we had wanted.

There were three races in the championships, the first being the Bairns Bucket which I was desperate to go in and win. I didn't. Contact with a pole halfway down spun me round and the time it took to sort myself out robbed me of the race. I ended up third behind Michael Hall-Hall and Alan Stewart. I was really brassed off. I had been determined to win my first race in Scotland and a silly error had defeated me. I resolved to make up for it in the slalom.

The second race, the giant slalom, was just too big for me. I was lost in the gates and ended up 38th, but this wasn't my event and I wasn't too disappointed. The slalom was my forte and it was the third and last of the races.

The race was won by Julian Vasey. Julian, a tall, curly-haired lad who lived in Switzerland and skied for the British team had great natural talent, and I had no chance against him. I skied the first run as well as I could though, and was not unhappy. In the second run

I again hit a pole and had to climb back up to the gate in order to finish the course. Despite this I was tenth overall and the fastest of the younger racers. To my mind this result avenged the defeat in the Bairns Bucket, and I was really happy. The only people ahead of me were either on the British team or on Scottish training camps. They were all a lot older than me and I felt I had put up a good show even though no one else seemed to be at all impressed with my efforts.

After these championships my brother and I decided that we should join one of the British racing clubs if we were going to continue improving. I wanted to join the St Moritz club because there was a nice redhead there, but Stefan vetoed this and opted for the Kandahar Club. It was a decision neither of us ever regretted.

The next three years followed pretty much the same pattern. I skied with the Kandahar club at their training sessions in Europe whenever I could and I worked on at school as the time for my O-levels drew closer. Every year I would ski the British championships and was able to improve steadily. The 1968 championships in Andermatt were cancelled because of the weather but in 1969 at Brand I won my age group and my self-confidence was on the up and up. I knew I was in the running for overall champion and set my sights on the 1970 races at Cairngorm.

On the basis of my 1969 results I was invited to the British Espoir training at Val d'Isère: my foot was in the door to the British team. Everything about this was new to me. It was my first time skiing in France, my first time with a French coach, Michel Rudigoz, and the first time I had had more than one pair of skis – one pair of which were 223cm Rossignol Allais Major downhill racing skis. For the first time I had the tools to do the job.

I knew everyone in the squad from the Junior Championships but there was one pair of skis, about twenty centimetres shorter than the rest, set aside for somebody called Willy Bailey: a name that none of us knew. This was, and is, unusual in ski racing. Skiing is a small world and everyone knows everyone else. This dark horse in the Espoir camp had us all intrigued, especially as his skis were so short. When we finally met him we could hardly believe it: he was a midget with bottle glasses. He didn't look as though he could ski the nursery slopes, let alone the downhill. But this little mouse turned out to be a tiger on the slopes. He really flew and his courage was ample insurance against ever being ribbed for his appearance. In time he became one of my greatest friends.

The French method of training at this camp did not impress me. Two weeks of being barked at by Michel Rudigoz was about as much as I could take. The resentment I built up against his style of training was partly offset by an opportunity to ski a downhill on the Val d'Isère championship course. The conditions were atrocious, it was snowing and the light was very flat, but I was determined to be the fastest of our group. As it turned out I was pipped into second place (yet again) by Jeremy Lyell. I have never been able to forget this, as every time I meet Jeremy now he rubs in his great triumph!

No sooner were the races over than I was back in the Hague at school. As usual I had missed the beginning of term but I arrived on the Monday morning (the last race had been on Sunday) to be greeted by my headmistress, Mrs Donaldson. It was my O-level year and she was concerned that my life was being taken up too much by skiing. If I didn't do well, she said, I would be beaten over the head with a ski stick. The pep talk over it was straight into the classroom for a maths exam – an exercise I found even more demanding than the downhill that was still fresh in my memory.

Despite the goals I had as a skier I knew that if I didn't do well at school I would have nothing to fall back on when the skiing was over, or if things didn't turn out as I hoped. The school was very academically-orientated, which was good for my head, but there was little emphasis on sport – only two hours a week – and to keep fit I cycled the ten kilometres each way to school. It did not get me fit enough, though, and when real fitness training started under a proper coach I found I had a long way to catch up.

Despite 'O' levels looming up in June the number one thing on my mind was the British Championships at Cairngorm in April. I went up with the Kandahar Club under the eyes of coaches Gusti Fischnaller and former Austrian team coach Hans Bosch (who today is the man responsible for Harti Weirather's racing skis). The club had arranged ten days preparation with the coaches and they were ten of the best training days I had ever had. Under their guidance my race technique improved considerably and when the races themselves came along I felt I was ready.

The first race was the slalom and things couldn't have gone better. I won both legs and overall I was the winner by some three seconds. Naturally the win pleased me, especially as it was Willy Bailey chasing me home in second place, but I was racing for the money as much as the glory. Nestlés, the sponsors of the championships, had put up £150 as a training grant for the winner and I wanted it desperately. With that I would be able to get in some summer training on the Kaprun glacier – something I had always wanted to do but had never been able to afford.

Just winning the slalom, however, was not sufficient to get the money. I had to win the giant slalom as well, and of the three disciplines it was the one where my track record was the least impressive.

Once again everything fell into place. I started number two and skied as well as I had ever done. My time was never even approached. Stuart Fitzsimmons, who had vowed to beat me before the race, skied off the course and Willy Bailey crashed. As I had gone at number two I was able to watch the other runners from the bottom. Among the later starters a young skier caught my eye. He was not amongst the leaders but his skiing had a touch of class about it and I was impressed. He was Peter Fuchs – whom I still had to wait until the summer to meet.

The £150 was now mine and I could take it home, but the trophies I had to hand back. For some inexplicable reason the authorities refused to allow them to grace a mantelpiece in Holland. The precious objects had to remain on British soil: another lesson in my continuing education on the inflexibility of officials.

Driving away the next day we stopped somewhere for a cup of tea and I picked up a copy of *The Times*. Naturally I went first to the sports pages to see my name in print but I was surprised to see myself actually written up in a lengthy article by John Hennessy entitled *A Man Among Boys*. It was a fantastic fillip for my ego and my confidence. Hennessy, a professional journalist and a man who had seen many skiers, saw in me the seeds of a champion. His article reinforced my already strong faith in myself; it also made me think for the first time about the power of the press on the sport – I realised that the help of the press was important in the achievement of ambitions. Hennessy's praise made me want to conquer the world: everything seemed better and brighter after reading his piece than it had been before. But in the back of my mind I knew that if a good write-up could lift me, so a bad one could do the opposite. The high induced by that article was intoxicating and addictive.

The euphoria of those championships carried me through my 'O' levels. I sat the exams during an oppressively humid June, but had to wait until September for the results. When Mrs Donaldson came into our class with them I was sweating with nerves, looking to see if she had that ski stick in her hand. She saw my anxiety and smiled. I had done as well as I had hoped, nine subjects sat and nine subjects passed. It was the icing on the cake of a great year.

The next year, 1971, started off less encouragingly. Somehow I just couldn't get things to settle down. My skis refused to run with the sweetness they had shown at Cairngorm and my co-ordination had gone to pot. The despair generated by this bad patch wasn't helped by the training methods of Michel Rudigoz. In Willy Bailey and myself he had two young boys whose keenness was razor-sharp, but Rudigoz never seemed to recognise it or encourage it. Skiing under him was like having cold water poured onto your ambitions. It was a waste – both Willy and I wanted something better. We had a lot to give and Rudigoz seemed unable to capitalise on it. For the first time I began to experience the real horror of frustration.

This frustration was still with me in January at Caspoggio, where I was entered for my very first race on the International Skiing Federation circuit. I was in the slalom with a start number of one hundred and forty-five. That meant a wait of two-and-a-half hours before I could go, and when I did it was nearly dark and the ruts in the course were like trenches. Needless to say I fell over at about gate twelve and came down to earth with a rush. I realised then that there was a hell of a long way to go.

The following week was my World Cup debut. As I was a Kandahar Club member I had been squeezed into the Arlberg Kandahar races: a giant slalom at Crans Montana and a slalom at Mürren.

For the first time I was skiing amongst the big names. There on the start list, along with names like Henri Duvillard, Jean-Noël Augert and Karl Schranz, at start number seventy-four was 'Bartelski'. Unlike the top boys, however, I was my own technician and it was while preparing my skis for the first of the races that I noticed

I had scraped them down so much there was no groove left. As I had no back-up skis it was either ski without grooves, or not ski at all. As it turned out it didn't matter. In the giant slalom I made my by now customary debut, and fell onto my nose.

Things were a little better at Mürren for the slalom. Skiing in my downhill suit with a sweater over the top as I had no slalom trousers, I managed to get down without falling over and finished in twenty-fifth place. Perhaps this doesn't sound too bad – but, unfortunately, only twenty-six skiers finished the race, the only person behind me being red-headed Scot Iain Finlayson. The agony of it all was not that we were last, but the margin by which we were last. The gap between us and the rest of the field was more than the gap between twenty-fourth and the winner. I felt acutely embarrassed. But to my amazement some of the British officials actually congratulated me for having finished. I was stunned and perplexed: I was being congratulated for a humiliating defeat. I felt I had to go away and check my dictionary to find the real meaning of the word 'competing'. I couldn't understand why the British were even in the game if all they wanted me to do was finish. I wanted to win; they just wanted me not to fall down. I was disgusted.

With a sour taste in my mouth I returned to school; a place of which I was now seeing less and less. It was my A-level year and the work was tougher, but skiing was making the terms shorter and shorter. It was February when I got back to school after the Mürren race and I planned to be away again in April for the last races of the season. When the time came I telephoned Michel Rudigoz to find out where I should go and what races I should do. He retorted: 'Don't bother.' His attitude was that as there were only a few races left it wasn't worth making the effort. Despite him I 'bothered' anyway. I checked the schedule and found that the team was at Les Diablerets in Switzerland for a FIS giant slalom race on Les Mosses. The first run was encouraging considering that I had been practising with school books rather than slalom gates – I finished close on the heels of the A-team members, Royston Varley and Alex Mapelli-Mozzi.

The second run was in the afternoon and was preceded by lunch. It was a fabulous day and we all sat in the sun on a restaurant terrace and enjoyed the food and wine. A few glasses of wine had me feeling really good and I was looking forward to the afternoon race but, when I looked over at the Austrian team, I noticed that the drinking had been getting out of hand. Two of their team members in particular, Werner Bliener and Alfred Matt, were absolutely blotto. On the course inspection Werner Bliener actually had to be held up to get him safely down the course. Astonishingly, though, Bliener still managed to come fourth in the race. I could hardly believe it. Here was I, after hard training and considerable application, happy to have collected sixty-four FIS points on my way to the next goal, selection for the 1972 Olympics, while a drunken Austrian, without apparent effort, could sail into fourth place in a field not lacking in talent. I realised then that there was a lot more to skiing than met the eye.

This result, and a similar one I was to collect in a later race, put me in fourth place in the British rankings and, as there were to be four members in the British team for the Sapporo Olympics in Japan, I felt it was logical that I would have a place. But logic does not appear to dominate the thinking of skiing administrators. Instead of just sending the four best, they decided that a Scot had to be included in the team – and the top four in the ranking were Julian Vasey, Alex Mapelli-Mozzi, Royston Varley and myself, all Englishmen.

Unfortunately the problem was solved by tragedy. While we were training at Lotschental Julian Vasey had a bad accident and ruined an Achilles tendon. It was a disaster for him and I felt his disappointment deeply. Of all the members of the team Julian was the one with the most natural talent. He was not from an upper-class background – his skiing prowess had developed from being brought up in Switzerland – but he had all that it took. The accident to his tendon led him to retire on the spot – a decision that I felt was a real shame as, partly through the prejudices of some elements in British skiing, Julian had never really fulfilled his tremendous potential. He was a happy-go-lucky fellow and was known as 'the hippy' on the squad but, after his retirement, he changed his image completely and became a pin-striped-suit-wearing stockbroker. Sadly he was eventually killed in a motorcycle accident on 27 May 1977: my birthday.

Julian's retirement opened the way for me to get into the team. I drove back to London with Iain Finlayson, the Scot who filled the fourth berth in the squad, and we enjoyed the novelty of being kitted out in our Olympic finery. There was a sort of 'electric' midnight blue nylon winter coat (not, I thought, a coat that would ever see the light of day in London) and beige slacks and jumpers. For some peculiar reason, however, we were not supplied with blazers – a great disappointment – and the maroon and white racing suits were a little too thick and not very close fitting. The only piece of kit I really liked were the racing sweaters – cobalt blue with a Union Jack on the sleeve. I liked this Union Jack, not only because of patriotism but because it symbolised the purpose of our mission. We were representing Britain, skiing for our country. Previous successes and failures had been mine alone. Now I had my country riding along with me. I felt the responsibility deeply and was determined not to let anyone down.

There was nothing particularly noteworthy about the journey. Our little midnight-blue-swathed band flew BOAC 707 to Moscow and then on to Tokyo. At seventeen I was still the shrimp of the squad (of the skiers, only Valentina Iliffe in the girls' squad was younger than me) and I was the one most awed by the importance of the occasion. The others cavorted on the journey rather as if they were going away on holiday, not athletes about to compete for their country. I was somewhat taken aback by this, but not as much as I was to be when we finally got to Sapporo.

I shared a room with Royston Varley in a comfortable Japanese-style apartment. I was impressed by the atmosphere in the village: for me it was fascinating. Athletes from all over the world, ice skaters, ski jumpers, ice-hockey players, bob sleighers, all mingled in a good natured and convivial, though apparently chaotic, mêlée. Because there were so many athletes and so many teams it was necessary to stagger meal-times and training times. This meant that the village was always bustling and I was caught up in the atmosphere of endeavour. It was stimulating being among so many people with a common goal – to do the best they could for their country.

The pageantry of the opening ceremony and the emotion that it generated was almost overpowering for me. I couldn't help thinking about the millions watching on television and the music, the pomp, the noise and the colour all helped to fill me with pride. The great high that I felt on the march-past made me think that anyone who wasn't lifted and inspired to good performances by this intoxicating euphoria must be really cold inside. On that day I began to realise what the Olympic ideal was all about. Here were the Russians and the Americans, the British and the Germans competing together for fun and the glory of sport. Politics were forgotten, on that parade there were only athletes ready to test their skills against others. Unfortunately it didn't take me long to realise that the great amateur principle that sport was more important than politics did not hold true in practice. I soon came face to face with the bitter hatreds and rivalries that lay just under the surface.

For me, the worst example of this involved the hero of my early days and the man who had first spotted my potential – Karl Schranz. At this time Avery Brundage, the president of the International Olympic Committee, was cracking the whip about 'shamateurism' in sport. For him the only amateur was the man who worked from nine to five and did his sport in his own time and at his own expense. It was, of course, an unrealistic view, but he held it passionately and was determined to find a scapegoat in an attempt to drive the semi-professionals from the amateur sport movement. Unfortunately that scapegoat was Karl Schranz.

At thirty-three, Schranz was no youngster in the sport but he had put up some great performances in practice and was one of the favourites for the race. Suddenly he was on his way home with his knuckles rapped, barred from competing in the Olympics. The IOC had determined that Schranz had stepped over the line that delineated amateur sport and they sacked him. I was shocked. Even my own limited successes had been achieved at the expense of school work and I knew that, if I was to rise any higher in the sport, I would have to devote even more time to it – in effect become more professional.

The irony of the expulsion of Schranz was that, when he finally arrived back home in Austria, the whole country turned out to welcome him as a hero. For them he wasn't a naughty boy returning in disgrace but a great sportsman who had been victimised by blind officialdom. He could hardly have received a more rapturous welcome on his return had he arrived back with the gold medal.

In Sapporo the Olympic ski races were held on a sulphur-belching volcano and the smell was sometimes nauseating – incongruous really, as the surrounding scenery of mountains and lakes was very beautiful and conveyed a freshness that had no room for a smell similar to that of a room full of men who had all had a good curry the night before. It was surprising how soon I got used to the stench as I got down to my own preparation for the races. But I felt lost. I desperately wanted to do well but I didn't know how to do so. I saw the other teams with their back-up facilities, masseurs, doctors, coaches and the like, and I wondered where mine were. I had neither help nor guidance, at least when compared with the affluent teams, and I felt cheated. It was like being in a bus station and wanting to go as far as possible but not knowing which bus to take and without the money to buy a ticket anyway.

This was reflected in my performances. In the downhill I was forty-third, ten seconds behind the winner but third of the Brits and two seconds ahead of Iain Finlayson (so justifying my place in the team). The giant slalom was on a course so steep that we all fell on the first run but I continued to try and I continued to train. I didn't notice this amongst the other members of the British squad. As the team midget I expected to have an example of application and dedication set to me by the older and senior members. But I didn't. It seemed to me that they were more interested in the cheap cameras in the shops than doing well in the races.

On slalom day, when I received my race number from Richard Berry, the men's team manager, I was shocked to see that I had been drawn for the group of contestants who had no FIS points. I had expected to be drawn higher up, with skiers who had qualifying points, but, for some reason, the officials had put me amongst the last group of sixteen, of whom I was the only one with qualifications. It seems trivial, I know, to worry about such a minor thing. I might, after all, have had a start number only a few places higher even if I had been drawn from the qualified runners – but we had team officials there to look after us, and whose job it was to see that we had the best, and they hadn't bothered. The effect on me was momentous. When you are young and keen and trying to learn, you need to feel your efforts and achievements are appreciated and understood. I had paid my dues with the FIS races in Europe and I had won my points the hard way. Now my team management couldn't even be bothered, apparently, to see that I got my entitlement in the starting line-up for the race. For me that was another lesson.

On the flight back to Britain I was the only skier (the others had gone to Hong Kong for a shopping trip) and I had plenty of time to think. I was sitting next to John Curry for some of the way and I learned how much time and effort he had to put into his sport to stay among the world's best. I came to realise that if I was to make it, my approach would have to be altered. I would have to become more single-minded and aggressive. I didn't know how to go about that, and I didn't know who to do it with, but I did know that to be success-ful I had to accept more of the responsibility myself. Nobody wanted me to win more than I did. If I was to succeed I would have to find a way that allowed me to be more independent and less hog-tied by the petty restrictions and frustrations that were so much a part of the sport's desk-bound administration.

THE THREE
MUSKETEERS

Going it alone and flying above the tangle of traps and snares laid by sports officials for the punishment of their less obedient charges is never easy. Fortunately I had Willy Bailey, by now a firm friend and collaborator, on my side: and with Peter Fuchs we made up 'The Three Musketeers'.

It had taken me a long time to meet up with Peter, but this was achieved at the Outward Bound School at Aberdovey in Wales just a few months before the Sapporo Olympics. We hit it off immediately. At one stage the school leaders, grinning with the jovial sadism common to all such schools, armed us with tents and sleeping bags and loaded us into trucks for a twenty mile drive into the wilderness. Before getting into the truck I asked Peter to duck inside and get three green handkerchiefs from my locker. He immediately picked up the wink that I gave him as I made the request and came back out to the truck with the 'handkerchiefs' – in reality three promises from the Bank of England to pay the bearer one pound – secure in his pocket. At the end of the drive we were unloaded, given a map, and sent on our way by the instructors, who waved goodbye and said sarcastically that they would see us for tea. They didn't really expect us until the following morning.

But Peter and I had our 'handkerchiefs'. We walked a short way to a nearby village, found a taxi and used the money to get us to within a mile or so of the school. The time it took us to walk this short distance had us arriving just as everyone else was about to have tea. I will always remember the look on their faces as we walked in the gate. They could not believe that we had completed the exercise in such a short time and Peter and I were in no hurry to tell them the secret. As far as the instructors were concerned, we were just superbly efficient map readers and walkers. In the end we did tell our fellow trampers, and the instructors, what we had been up to and it was a great joke – but for Peter and me it was something much more. It cemented the bonds of a friendship that was to be crucial to both our lives over the next few years. The rapport that we developed at that Outward Bound camp never left us. With Willy Bailey, Peter Fuchs and I were three of a kind. We were British skiers with the will to win at the highest level of competition the sport could offer and we were prepared to charge at the Holy Cow of Swiss and Austrian dominance – whatever the cost.

After Sapporo, Willy, Peter and I met up at Lotschental. It was sad that they hadn't been on the team (especially as they were a damn sight keener than a lot of those who were!) but our task was to show that we were the future. Willy managed to get 'team' jerseys made up for us so that we looked the part and a fourth was made for a trainer that Peter's father had been using at his Austrian Ski School at Cairngorm. His name was Dieter Bartsch.

The task for us now was the British Championships at Carr Bridge in Scotland in April, 1972. We made our way up there independently but arrived two weeks before the races and began moulding our joint assault. Those two weeks were extremely fruitful but we all had a feeling that the end was in sight for the British men's team. There was little enthusiasm for it in the Federation and we suspected it was about to be disbanded. Our enthusiasm for racing was undiminished, however. We wanted to go on and we had to work out a way of doing it by ourselves. Sacrifices would have to be made, and we knew there would be hardships, but we also knew that we had to do the job properly and with dedication. We couldn't afford to do it any other way – if we were going to make all the races and perform to the best of our abilities we had to show a collective resolve that no British 'team' had shown before.

The talks that we had together in that fortnight were, in effect, battle plans. We had common goals and great dreams. There was no acrimony and no disagreement. Slowly and painstakingly we put together the bricks and mortar that would allow our little company to take to the ski road.

Those British Championships were good for us. For the first time foreign racers had been asked to compete but, of the British racers, Peter managed to win the giant slalom, with me second, and I took the slalom. The result gave me the overall championship, which was very pleasing. When the three of us met up in the piano room of the Fuchs' home after the races we knew we were on the right track. All we needed was the money.

The first day that we would all meet up again, 20 June, 1972, was set as the start of our 'official' association. Willy was in charge of equipment, Peter looked after the programme, while I was to oversee the economic and political side of the operation. After very detailed assessments of the costs of a year in the ski circus I decided we would each need to put in £700 if we were going to be at all effective. That £2,100 was to include the purchase of a vehicle which would not only transport us from race to race but also serve as hotel and ski workshop. At this stage none of us was old enough to hold a European driving licence but that day was not far off. We knew that without such a vehicle our efforts would be doomed from the start.

Getting the money from our parents was the easiest part. As we were to be on the road for so long the amount we needed was only about the same as they would have to pay if we were living at home. In fact we ended up with a total of £2,500 and I started the search for a suitable van. Before very long I found a cream Volkswagen bus that took about a third of the budget and we began to convert it.

Just as important as money was the vital ingredient of publicity. I knew from personal experience of the John Hennessy article how lifting good press could be, and I was keen to see that the efforts of our team came to the attention of the British public. It was with this in mind that I spoke to John Samuel, the sports editor of *The Guardian*. John, who was then and still is today, one of the most avid and erudite supporters of winter sports, wrote an article in his paper that really set us up. In effect, it was our launching. The public now knew about us and our plans. We were committed: like the cavalry in the westerns, now it was either death or glory.

The van – our hotel-cum-transport – did not prove easy to convert. The tiny space inside had to sleep three people, and hold all the skis and gear necessary for a full winter on the road, together with all the spares needed for roadside repairs. We did this work ourselves in the main although my father helped to get the van roadworthy and my brother Stefan painted a huge Union Jack on the roof to identify us. Now all we needed was for one of us to get a licence so that we could get the show on the road.

For any athlete, however, it is no good heading for the top of the mountain if you are going to run out of puff halfway up. We had to get fit; fitter than we had ever been before. Dieter Bartsch, our trainer, had a house in St Johann am Tauern in Austria and Peter and I (Willy was to join us later) went there for a month of very intensive fitness training. Dieter allowed no let-up. Long-distance walking in the hills, running, and general exercise work, was the order of the day from dawn until dusk. The only breather we were allowed was an hour of rest immediately after lunch. By the time that month was over we were literally jumping out of our skins.

While we were at Dieter's I had written to the Ski Federation in London telling them of our plans and keeping them up to date with our progress. I also heard that the Australian Federation had offered facilities and accommodation for a month's training for two British racers, provided that each put up £100. Peter and I were very keen to go. It presented a perfect opportunity to round off the rigorous training at Dieter's with some work on snow. However, the Federation ruled that another British racer, Scot Fraser Clyde, had to have one of the two berths available. Again it was my father who stepped in to help out. His position as a senior captain with KLM meant that he could get me a cheap flight to Australia, so enabling me to join Peter and Fraser at Thredbo and Falls Creek in the Snowy Mountains. Although I qualified for the concession through my father's job, it was not without its problems. All such cheap travel is on a stand-by basis. If the plane fills up with fare-paying passengers it is the stand-by people who are the first to be dumped. Flying ten thousand miles on stand-by, with the nagging possibility of being stranded in Singapore, definitely adds to the grey hair count. Fortunately this trip presented no problems and I got there without trouble, virtually bunny-hopping Peter all the way. He was on a regular QANTAS flight that was either landing as I was taking off or vice versa. We landed in Sydney at about the same time but he was a lot less hassled than I was!

We both picked up some FIS points in our first race at Falls Creek but while training for the second Peter had an argument with a pole and damaged an Achilles tendon. Unfortunately this injury was never adequately diagnosed or treated and it was to bother him for the rest of his racing career.

For me, getting back to England was no easier on the nerves than the flight out. I knew there were likely to be problems with fare-paying passengers at Singapore and Karachi, so I had made arrangements with my father to join up with an aircraft he was flying at Melbourne. There was no room on this aircraft either but I flew in the cockpit as an extra – not the most comfortable way to travel! It is worth pointing out here that all this travel took considerable thought and planning. My father made special efforts for me but things were never able to happen with clockwork efficiency. I always had deadlines and schedules to meet – on this occasion I had to be in Holland for a driving test or face the possibility of a three-month wait for another – and the travel always presented unforeseen problems. If I had ten pounds for every hour I have sat up studying airline timetables in an attempt to get somewhere on time I would be the richest of ski racers: certainly we could have replaced the ancient VW with a far grander motor home.

The day after getting home I took and passed my driving test and set off almost immediately to pick up Peter at Munich airport for the drive to Kaprun for training. We were in high spirits. This was it – the start of the great adventure. We were still slapping each other on the back as I drove away in the bus but I was brought down to earth with a jolt when my lack of full attention caused me almost to run over a dog. For such a new young driver it was a big shock and it was a much more serious Bartelski who settled down to the long drive to Austria.

Willy, meanwhile, was finishing his schooling at Lausanne and arranging for clothing and equipment for us. He had done a great deal of work in putting our case to ski manufacturers and, after a week staying in a barn and training with the Kandahar Club at Kaprun, Peter and I headed for Geneva to visit some of these factories and to see Willy.

As usual we didn't have much time to play with. Willy had set up appointments for us and we were going to have to move to make them but Lady Luck – who so often seems to have gone out to lunch when I am around – let us down again. On the motorway just before Salzburg blue smoke began to fill the driving cab and the motor started sounding more like a single cylinder Seagull outboard than a motor-car engine. Concerned, we stopped at the nearest garage, only to be told that it was a full mile to the nearest VW specialist. Fortunately it was mostly downhill and we were able to coast on the motor but, just as we were turning into the garage yard, the engine wheezed, coughed and exploded. It seized solid and we had a dead car on our hands. The garage men were just locking up for lunch but the foreman told us to come back in an hour and he would see what he could do. When we returned he told us that he had one reconditioned engine which he could let us have for £150. Relieved, we agreed, and Peter rushed off to change some money while I stayed with the van. The men in that garage were magnificent. Only an hour and a half after they returned from lunch we were back on the road heading once again for our appointments, the only difference being that now we were running in a new engine. Old Lady Luck was in a peculiar and fickle mood that day.

First stop was the Kneissl factory. I had been skiing on Kneissl for about a year but I had chosen the skis largely because Karl Schranz, still a great hero to me, was associated with them. Peter, on the other hand, had a preference for Kastle as a Kastle serviceman had worked for his father at the Austrian Ski School in Scotland.

Both factories gave each of us six pairs of skis. That was more than either of us had ever had before. Normally, the factory people would not have countenanced requests for help from young lads travelling Europe in a beat-up VW – but they knew we were serious. They knew that Peter and I had been to Australia for training and they knew that we had made arrangements to train with the Austrian 'C' team. As we left the Kastle factory with our twelve pairs of skis in the back of the van we were happy indeed. Getting them was a major landmark, a giant step down the road towards our goals.

But the joy was tempered by physical tiredness. Driving a minibus on mountain roads is a big strain and a tremendous responsibility, so as soon as we saw a suitable field off the road we drove in to it for the night. Peter was the cook of the band and he began to prepare our supper on a ski-waxing Primus at the back of the van while I refreshed myself with a wash from the water we stored in large plastic containers. It was our first real night on the road, and one that I will never be able to forget. There we were, two young lads with shared interests, eating and sleeping under the stars without a care in the world. We didn't care what anyone thought of us, we were doing what we wanted; we couldn't have felt better.

After supper, sitting round the Primus, we began to talk about the problem of bindings – after all, twelve pairs of new skis were no use at all unless we had something to hold them on to our boots. The thought occurred to us that perhaps we should all use the same binding. We could drive to the Salomon factory at Annecy and maybe even pick up some sponsorship or even a contribution towards the petrol costs of our travels.

Excited at the prospect, but knowing it was a gamble, we picked up Willy in Lausanne and headed for Salomon. We arrived in the office of Jean-Lou Sarbach, the Salomon racing boss, with high hopes but nothing to sell apart from our enthusiasm. We did, however, have Willy: and that was no mean asset. Willy was one of those people that nobody can refuse. He would cock his head on one side and look up soulfully from behind his fish-eye glasses, melting the hardest of hearts. He put our case to Jean-Lou with great passion. We would ski exclusively on Salomon bindings as The Three Musketeers, determined to do the very best we could for our sponsor. It didn't sound like much – we seemed to be asking an awful lot for virtually nothing – but Jean-Lou was impressed. He thought over our request and agreed, on condition that we put Salomon advertising on the van.

That night, four of us (Fiona Sutton, a girlfriend of mine who lived in Geneva, had come down to stay for the night) spent the night in the van somewhere outside Annecy in a mood of great expectation. The next day we were to become 'professional'.

The Salomon deal supplied us with equipment and a cheque for 3,500 francs for the advertising on the bus. We now had all the equipment we needed – all we had to do was look the part.

Although we were beginning to get the support and co-operation of equipment manufacturers, and we were on the way to becoming accepted in the racing business itself, we were still teenage boys with teenage desires. Throughout history teenage boys have been interested in clothing and style, and we were no different. In skiing the way you are dressed is an indication to the competition of how seriously you take your own challenge and how seriously others value your potential. We therefore began a series of 'raids' on clothing manufacturers in order to be as impressively turned out as possible.

A trip to Pull Montant, a ski sweater manufacturer in Annecy who supplied the French team, produced four blue sweaters with multi-coloured striping down the arms (one of which my father still skis in). Another visit, this time to the Cébé factory, resulted in our being equipped with massive supplies of goggles and sunglasses – no small item, as these enabled us to reward favours with the gift of a pair of sun glasses, which in turn helped to bolster our burgeoning 'professional' image.

Indeed, the success we had with the acquisition of clothing had a greater importance than just the inflation of our personal egos. Although Peter and I were training with the Austrian 'C' team we both had girlfriends in Geneva (and Willy was still at school in Lausanne) so we took every opportunity to make the trip to Geneva. Every time we did this we always stopped off at some company or other on a 'raid'. A few sweaters here, a few sets of racing pants there, may not sound much, but each time we arrived back at Dieter's house we displayed the 'trophies' with considerable glee. This wasn't an unhealthy delight in personal aggrandisement but rather happiness that we were able to do something, however small, for Dieter. We were not in a position to pay him anything like what he was worth as a trainer and he was making considerable sacrifices on our behalf. The loot we brought home was, in our small way, a thank-you to Dieter.

On the skiing front things were going better for Peter than for me. We were grateful to the Austrian 'C' team for letting us train with them, especially as it helped us keep our own training costs down, but Peter seemed to be getting more out of it than I was. We were concentrating on the slalom at this stage and, while Peter seemed to be flying, I was struggling just a little in his wake. If he hadn't been there I am quite sure I would have been too miserable to make the most of it but, being rivals as well as friends, his success was a spur to me. As a team, this was our advantage. We were never equal – always one of us was doing better than the other, making the one trailing pull up his socks and come back. Neither of us could bear to be the one left behind so we were always pushing ourselves hard to get ahead. But although we used each other to drive ourselves to better performances, we never carried our rivalry off the ski slope. When we were in Geneva we would go to parties and the cinema together more as brothers than as competitors. For both of us it was a time of excitement and stimulation. We were doing our own thing and London was a million miles away – our skiing was improving, our friendship was deepening, and we were content. We knew it could not last forever, but while it was happening we enjoyed every second. In some ways it was the calm before the storm, but you don't put on weatherproofs when the sun is still shining!

The thing now was for us to test ourselves. Peter and I had put in six months of solid training – more non-stop skiing in fact than either of us had ever done in our lives before. We were fit, and, although not expecting miracles, we were looking forward to seeing where we stood against the Swiss and Austrians. We were also looking forward to getting together as a foursome. Willy was just finishing his autumn term at school and Dieter, who had been cooling his heels slightly while Peter and I were with the Austrians, was keen for the four of us to put our money where our mouths were and take to the race circuit. The time had finally come when we would see if dedicated application and hard training paid dividends on the race track.

Our first attack as the Three Musketeers plus one was a FIS slalom competition at Courchevel in France. We left Austria in the van, Salomon advertising gleaming on the side and Union Jack proudly displayed on the roof, to pick up Willy and begin the real business of our lives – racing. None of us was hoping for a great deal, at least not openly, and we didn't get it. We were gathering points, particularly in the slalom, but it was a slow, uphill grind. I was quite pleased with my own acquisition of FIS points and, although I was still light years from being in the frame, I could measure my improvement week by week.

Our application and willingness to put up with any hardship in order to race gained us respect from the other racers. We had become, in effect, a ski country. Wherever there was a race our van was there too. It was as common a sight as the brightly-coloured company and team back-up vans and it told everyone that we did not intend to give up. This was the time when some of the strong alpine nations began to realise that the British men were, at last, making a serious attempt to breach their walls.

Despite our lack of actual race success in the FIS arena we were very hopeful of sweeping the field at the British championships which that year were being held in Flaine. We knew we had trained well and we knew that there was nobody among the British men who should have presented any serious challenge. But over-confidence is its own enemy and we bombed it. Peter's tendon trouble was flaring up again and Willy and I both crashed in the slalom. I managed to win the giant slalom but the overall title went to Stuart Fitzsimmons. We left Flaine with our tails between our legs. It was a lesson we needed. In ski racing nothing can be taken for granted, and soon we were back on the road, disappointed but undaunted.

The next step for me was a leap into the unknown. Peter had to spend some time recuperating and Willy wanted to enter a series of slalom races but I, on the advice of Dieter, entered my first World Cup downhill at Kitzbühel. The object was not so much an attempt at winning but rather a reduction in my FIS points. In international ski racing the points are rather like a golfer's handicap; the less points you have, the better skier you are – the points being assessed by the number of seconds you are behind the race winner. My target was to get fifty points or less. This would mean that the race organisers would start assisting me with accommodation costs, which would be a great help to our overall budget.

The Hahnenkamm at Kitzbühel was chosen for my attempt because I knew the course so well. This was where I had found my ski legs with Gitti Schatz and where Karl Schranz had first commented on my potential. It seemed the logical place to start serious downhilling.

Dieter and I arrived in Kitzbühel in the third week of January, 1973, to astonishment from the other teams. Typical of that reaction was a comment from the Kastinger boot serviceman who said: 'What the hell are you doing here? You don't race a downhill all year and then you turn up at the toughest!'

It was certainly a crazy thing to be doing. We had done little downhill training and we were going in cold against people who had devoted all their energies to the discipline. But, if I was to get my FIS points down, this was the last chance. The Hahnenkamm was the final race before the new FIS list came out – it was either race at Kitzbühel or keep my existing points ranking until the next listing sometime in March. I didn't want to wait that long.

In the event I failed. I simply wasn't up to it, and the course shook me around like a ball in a pin-ball machine. I managed to finish the race but more by good luck than good management. At one stage my body actually hit the ground but somehow I managed to bounce back onto my skis and struggle through to the finish. I didn't reduce my FIS points and I didn't do anything for my confidence. Indeed both Dieter and I were relieved when we were back in the bus heading for the less demanding races of the FIS circuit. I was down to earth again.

The following months saw us racing and racing and racing. If there was a race on somewhere we were there. It seemed that we were either racing, or driving to a race. On many occasions we raced in four countries within a week. It was exhausting in every way, but somehow it was also one of the high spots of our lives. Every waking thought (when we were not thinking of our girlfriends, that is) was devoted to achieving more speed, acquiring more skills, and making it to a resort in time for the start. We were all busier than we had ever been but, in our eyes at least, things were beginning to come together.

The final races of the year were two downhills at Zell am See in Austria. In the first Peter had a good run but I made some mistakes and finished down the field. In the second race, however, I started to get things right. I finished with a FIS points-score of thirty-two, reducing my ranking from the fifties into the thirties, a double jump – and I was thus able to look forward to the next season with an overall FIS score of thirty-eight. It wasn't the miracle I had hoped for, but it was in the right direction and I was more than happy.

Throughout much of this year only Peter and I had raced together: Willy had had to spend much of his time at school. Now it was my turn. My 'A' level exams were just two months away and I enrolled in a London crammer to immerse myself in Applied Maths and Physics.

In some ways it was like a holiday. The mental work was the complete opposite of the strenuous physical activity I had been used to, and I actually enjoyed the change. The intensity of the crammer work stimulated me and the two months passed in a flash. I sat the exams in June and, even before they were over, was looking forward to meeting up with Peter and Willy at the Fuchs' house at

Carrbridge to tone myself up and get into the hurly-burly of skiing again: this time with just a little help from the Federation.

At the beginning of the 1973 season the British Federation's Alpine Committee Chairman, Scot Ian Stevens, had decided to start assisting with Dieter's costs provided that we allowed Stuart Fitzsimmons and Alan Stewart to train with us. We were a little reluctant – after all, we were a small, close band who had gone through much hardship together and we felt ourselves to be a unit – but we could not refuse. Without the Federation's help we could not have met Dieter's expenses and he was crucial to our continued improvement; to have lost Dieter would have been a very severe blow indeed. So Stuart and Alan became part of our troupe, but only if they arranged their own transport. Our van was already bursting at the seams and the accommodation of two more bodies was quite simply impossible.

Thus it was an expanded group of skiers who began the 1973–74 training at Carrbridge. At first I struggled badly. The enforced lay-off at the crammer had softened my muscles and I spent the first few evenings so stiff I was hardly able to walk, but slowly, with the aid of Dieter's no-let-up, five-and-a-half-hour-day training programme (and the wonderful facilities that the Fuchs family made available to us) I began to get the steel back into my thighs.

Before long another young man joined us. While on the FIS circuit the previous year Peter had met up with a young Canadian that he liked. The lad had non-stop enthusiasm and an equally non-stop tongue but, when he came up to Carrbridge to join us, we all found him easy enough to get along with despite having to wander off into the woods on occasions just to get away from his constant prattle. So it was that I met Ken Read – the beginning of a friendship that is as strong today as it was tenuous then. He never became a member of our little group (after all, he had the might of the Canadian team to fall back on) but for the next ten years of my career he was my friend; one of the few people on the World Cup circuit whom I could trust and rely on implicitly.

That year Australia was out of the question, we just couldn't afford it, so we headed for the glacier at Dachstein for our summer training. Here we found a small hotel that let us live under the eaves in a large room for the equivalent of £2 a day full board, and we settled down to work on the snow again. Alan Stewart and Stuart Fitzsimmons arrived late. They had managed to acquire a rattling, run-down Bedford van for their travelling and they drove out in this, though they had considerable difficulty keeping the thing going. When they arrived at Dachstein the rest of us fell about laughing. Here were Alan and Stuart in a monstrous old vehicle that grunted and groaned, hissed and popped; it had no heating – they had to wedge sleeping bags into the doors in a vain attempt to keep warm – and was about as reliable as the Hesketh team in its formula one racing year. To us it was a joke. Ski racing requires almost constant travel, and for Alan and Stuart to be relying on that heap was stretching optimism just a little bit too far.

All the same the lot of us, including Ken Read, got down to training with a vengeance. In the slalom Ken and Peter, particularly Peter, were flying. He was going so well that the Austrian juniors would come over each day just to watch him. He was skiing like a dream, sailing through the gates and going really fast with superb style and minimum effort. He motivated us all. My own slalom was coming along in leaps and bounds and we all felt we were getting maximum benefit from the glacier.

When we were not skiing, we either went down to Dieter's home for some dry land exercises or off to find some distracting amusement. Sometimes we would decide to go go-karting, but Fitzy would always respond with: 'Nay mon, ah kanna afford it – ah'm stony-broke.' This happened every time, but pass an ice-cream shop and Stuart was immediately inside getting outside the biggest confection the shop could devise!

At other times we would hop in the van and head south to the sea for a couple of days. There was no question of affording a hotel so we would find a suitable beach and just park. It was a lazy, beach-comber's style of life, but ideally suited to our tissue-thin wallets. We would frolic on the beach and bask in the sun (and maybe even chat up a few ladies!) before heading back to the serious business of skiing.

It was a great time. All of us could feel the drive and the conviction of the others. We bolstered each other and, by the time that summer training was over, we knew we were as ready as we could be.

Willy, once again, had been magnificent in getting us clothing.

He had managed to talk the Steffner company, who made the jerseys for the Norwegian and Liechtenstein teams, into making us sweaters in the colours of Barclays Bank in recognition of a grant of £500 the bank had given us towards our costs. He also acquired some splendid downhill suits: the first time we had had the proper gear for this event.

It was also this year that we got our first proper downhill training. Literally on a shoestring we went to Haus, near Schladming, and stayed in a hostel alongside the top cable car station. Here, for about £2 a day, we survived on glutinous rice pudding flavoured with chocolate powder, while we practised on a downhill course that had virtually no snow. We didn't get much chocolate powder to sweeten the otherwise inedible rice, but there was more of it than there was snow on the track. For this training we were really stretching pound notes – this was living within the budget *par excellence.*

Despite the lack of snow we set to work building a course. With shovels we shifted what little snow there was to build jumps and turns that would approximate to the sort of conditions we were likely to find in a proper race. Unfortunately we got carried away with one of the jumps. The take-off slope was too steep and, when I skied it, I came down heavily on the back of my skis and only just avoided an accident. Behind me Stuart Fitzsimmons was sailing down the course completely oblivious of my near-miss. We all waved at him to try to stop him, but he thought we were waving him on to even greater speed and he hit the jump at about 55mph. It was like being rocketed straight into the air. He went up and up and up and then came crashing down with his skis virtually perpendicular to the slope. He was hurt, we didn't know how badly, but the rest of the day was spent getting him to a hospital. As it turned out he had cracked a vertebrae and was lucky not to have broken his back. The accident took the edge off our pleasure in the home-grown downhill run, but we shovelled the jump down a little and carried on with the training.

Stuart was in hospital at Schladming but, after a few days, signed himself out and headed for home with a plaster cast on his neck. To this day he says the reason for his early departure from the hospital was that we had left him with just one Neil Young cassette tape. On this Neil was wailing away on his *Harvest* album with lyrics like . . .

'I saw the needle and the damage done, a little part of it in everyone' ...
and Stuart was being driven quietly up the wall with depression.
Had we left him with some Rod Stewart, it might have been a
different story!

The downhill practice was obviously very useful to me but all the
practice in the world is no good if you haven't got the skis to do the
job on race day. I therefore made the trip to Kneissl to pick up a
couple of pairs of racing skis. I travelled to the factory alone, and
sat in the office of Walter Perwein, the factory service man, as he
arranged for my skis. Eventually two pairs arrived and Walter set
one aside and said to me: 'Look after this pair ... use them only for
races.' I didn't really know why he said this. They looked every inch
identical to the others but I knew Walter must have had a reason for
making the suggestion. What was so special about those skis I will
never know, but Walter certainly knew his stuff. Those skis were
quick – much quicker than the other pair. It was yet another lesson
for me: good race skis are made in the factory. It is possible to make
slow skis go a little quicker with careful preparation and waxing but
they will not be winners. Winning skis are definitely born in the
factory – no amount of preening can make winners out of skis that
haven't got that special, almost indefinable, something. I was
beginning to realise that winning at skiing involved much more than
a simple desire to get down the hill fast.

In mid-December 1973 there was a World Cup downhill at Zell
am See. I raced on the skis Walter had suggested and skied with all
the energy and courage I could muster. At the bottom, after as
smooth a run as I had had in any race, I looked at the clock and
knew I was finally on the right path. I was twenty-fifth in a World
Cup downhill out of seventy-five starters: only fifteen places off a
World Cup point. I knew that if I could come twenty-fifth I could
just as easily come fifteenth or even fifth. In my own eyes this was
my arrival. The years of sweat, effort and tears were bearing fruit. I
was on my way: at least I had got to the stage of timing the distance
between myself and the winners with a stop-watch. The sand-timer
could be thrown away.

The next race was Schladming, one of the most difficult of the
downhill courses. On the first day of inspection the atmosphere in the
finish area was tense and reflective. We had seen a very steep, very

fast course with jumps over roads and difficult turns. Everyone was apprehensive about their prospects. After the first actual practice, however, the frowns of worry had given way to grins of relief. The course was fast and tricky but it was possible. There were no terrible accidents and most racers skied the course with flair. As the weather was sunny, making the snow a little tacky, really fast times were out of the question so the course was unable to hit us with its obvious traps. On the day of the race, though, things were very different. A cold clear night had left the course, once so slow and sticky, icy and lightning fast. It was so fast that on my way to the start Piero Gros, who went on to win the 1976 slalom gold medal, put his finger to his head as if to say 'you are just plain loco'. He could so easily have been right. Many of the top racers crashed and quite early on Peter ended up in the straw bales. I was luckier. I finished twenty-second (the winner being Franz Klammer, his first ever downhill win) and lowered my FIS standing sufficiently to allow me to start in the first group of fifteen in European Cup races and the second group in World Championships. It was a great Christmas present.

That year I spent Christmas at home in Holland – my first non-white Christmas for six years. It was wonderful to share the festive season with my family and it was good for me to be able to relax. For the first time I was really self-assured. When friends of the family and acquaintances asked me what I did for a living I could say 'ski racer' without any feeling of self-deception. I felt a little like a novice skier who had suffered the early agonies of ski school and the ignominy of repeated falls only to find that one morning he could do it; and could finally call himself a skier to his friends. I was now a ski racer. There was no doubt in my mind.

After Schladming my next target was La Foux d'Allos in the South of France. This was a European Cup downhill and Peter and I were both hopeful – we were starting in the first group for the first time. The course was outrageous, big jumps and steep walls, but despite this Peter was skiing it well in the practices. I was not doing so well, I had trouble with a sore knee and I wasn't getting into an effective rhythm. But on race day I really put my head down and went for it. I was a lot faster: in fact I was going into jumps so much faster that I saw parts of the course I had never seen in training. At the bottom the clock showed me nearly ten seconds quicker than my fastest practice run. Needless to say I was delighted. I waited for Peter to come down to see his time. He was quick too – only half a second slower than me. We were both in the top ten and in the points. Peter was eighth and I, for the first time in my career, had a place on the podium in third place.

The Austrian coach at this race was Sigi Bernegger. We didn't have a lot to say to each other at the time but, seven years later, in New Zealand, he recalled this race and said: 'You know we were really worried about you two English guys.' If only we had known that at the time. We were naturally pleased with what we had done but how much more delighted we would have been had we known that the Austrians had taken notice of us. If we had been aware that they took us as a serious challenge, we would definitely have been that much harder to stop.

Nobody was more delighted by our success than Willy. His own natural talents were in the gates of slalom and giant slalom courses and he had opted to go for those races on the European Cup circuit; but talent wasn't the only reason for his decision. His poor eyesight meant that the lenses in his glasses were very expensive items, and he simply could not afford the perpetual opticians' bills every time he shattered his spectacles in downhill falls. Even so he was going through a lean patch in his own specialities. A nagging pain in his back and a lapse in self-confidence had resulted in some mediocre performances for him. Our success was just the tonic he needed. We all knew that we operated best as a team, and Willy rejoined us with new enthusiasm.

Next stop was Pontresina in the Engadine for the World Championships on the slopes of Signal above St Moritz Bad. Willy, Peter and I stayed in the Hotel Schweitzerhof in Pontresina – the first time we had seen the inside of a luxury hotel for many a long day. It went to our heads. The waiter was a jolly, friendly, chap full of 'would you like some more ice-cream', 'would you like some fruit salad' etc. We could hardly believe it. We were being treated like lords and we wallowed in the unaccustomed four-star treatment – until, that is, the time came to pay the bill. Every extra we had had found its way to the final addition. We had been gullible, if not actually ripped off. For a while there was some worry that we might not be able to pay the bill but a good Samaritan, in the form of Robin Bailey from the

Alpbach Visitors Ski Club, stepped in and saved us from embarrassment. Robin was an English businessman who wanted to get something done for the British team. He was very anxious to help. It was ironic that his first assistance should be in the form of saving us from a winter of washing up in the Schweitzerhof!

The top part of the Signal downhill course was fairly flat with a series of 'S' bends to follow, but the bottom section was just one hair-raising jump after another. Even though there was a lot of snow Peter and I had our problems. We fell several times and in one fall Peter cut himself quite badly. I got off more lightly with bruised knees but neither of us was really in good enough condition for a race. Fortunately the weather turned really foul and the race was put off for a week, giving both of us more than enough time to recover. It was also fortunate that Kastinger had brought out a new boot a few weeks before. Normally it would be considered stupid to change a racing boot halfway through the season but the new boot was made of softer material around the shin and this took less of a toll on my damaged legs. I knew I was taking a risk changing boots but it was a case of skiing in the new boots with a chance or skiing in my old boots in pain. I opted for the chance.

For that chance to be realistic, however, I had to have my skis in tip-top condition as well. Every night Peter and I would lovingly prepare our skis for the following day's practice and then we would give them to Dieter to wax. The skis that Kneissl had said would be good ones were still just that. In one practice session I was actually fastest on the top section but I put this down to Dieter's skill at waxing. It never occurred to me to attribute this speed to good skiing and superb skis. Naively we were believing more in Dieter than we were believing in ourselves; even so we were going well and we were happy.

Although I was doing well on the top sections in the practices, Peter was skiing the course faster overall. He was really flying and it spurred me on. Despite being slower than him on full course times I felt that somewhere I had something in reserve, something that I could draw on when the chips were down.

On race day I was frozen with tension in the start gate. Nerves are common to all racers and they are necessary to allow the body to drive itself to the limit but, for this race, my nerves had virtually rendered me a cripple. Dieter almost had to chuck me out of the starting gate, but once I was on the course I put my head down and went.

Although this was the first time I had been in the second group in a World Championship race the old Bartelski luck seemed to be on the blink again. All second group starting places were drawn out of a hat and I could have had anything from sixteen to thirty – needless to say, I drew thirty. It was a curse. After twenty-nine racers had already been down, the track was badly rutted up and I hit one of the holes in the 'S' turns, over-rotated coming out of the traverse, and was off my line going into the next sharp left-hander. To compensate I forced myself down lower to keep my wind resistance to a minimum and allow myself to build up maximum possible speed for the big, bad, jumps to the finish.

As my skis went over the finish line I was an angry man. I thought I had blown it. Even when I saw the time clock flash up fifteenth place I continued to curse. I knew that I had botched it up and could have been even closer. Robin Bailey and John Samuel from *The Guardian* were patting me on the shoulders but I couldn't accept their enthusiasm. I felt I had let myself down.

Eight minutes later Peter's time came up on the scoreboard. He was nineteenth. More hands started to pat us on the shoulders but Peter, too, was unhappy. If anything his language was even worse than mine. His was a fine performance but I had pipped him. All week he had been consistently faster and now, in the race, he found himself taking a back seat. It was hard for him to take and I knew how he felt. After all, I had been in the same position often enough myself.

On the bus going back to the hotel Peter and I were still a bit low but Willy, with his typical good sense, put the whole thing into perspective. 'For goodness sake', he said, 'you have put two Brits into the top twenty of a World Championship. Even some of the Alpine countries haven't done that.' His attitude was that we had put British men's skiing amongst the big boys. It took me six years to realise that he was right.

— 4 —

THE BRICK WALL

In that magnificent year, 1974, we were young idealists making our way, slowly and not without setbacks, in a cynical and pragmatic world: yet we had started to see some healthy shoots growing from the seeds we had sown. What we didn't realise was that others could see those shoots as well. No sooner had our results at St Moritz reached the ears of the British ski authorities than we started getting offers of assistance from London. In our naivety we accepted them all. We were glad that at last people from home were taking an interest in us and, largely because the big league alpine teams did so well with the help and guidance they got from their own well-oiled Federation back-up machinery, we felt that well-directed help from home could do nothing but speed the realisation of our ambitions too. Little did we know that the halcyon days were gone: that the best organisation we ever had was as the band of self-motivated babes-in-the-wood we called the Three Musketeers. From the moment we let the authorities infiltrate our tight-knit circle we started a time-bomb that would end in our own destruction. Like Jack Kerouac in *On the Road*, the only way our team could survive was as free agents. Okay, so we made mistakes at times, and tilted at windmills, Don Quixote style, but we were happy, independent and optimistic. All we wanted was to see a Union Jack flying over a ski race winner's podium: but, from now on, we would spend more time competing against our 'helpers' than against the other racers.

The first offer of help came from Robin Bailey – the man who had saved us from a marathon dish-washing stint in Pontresina. There was no doubt about Robin's keenness, or his willingness to commit both his time and his resources to the team. We saw him as a sort of white knight riding in to carry our banner even higher. Robin's ideas were big. As a businessman, small thinking was anathema to him and he began conveying his ideas to the Federation Alpine

Committee in London. They must have been impressed because, before we knew it, Robin was appointed manager of the men's team.

From the start he was a ball of energy. The team was expanded – suddenly we found there were up to twelve boys in the squad – and bicycles were acquired as training aids. He arranged for two weeks physical training with the Parachute Regiment in Aldershot (which included a round in the ring with a mountainous Army bruiser!) and he set up wind tunnel tests to help us adopt the correct aerodynamic position for fast downhill running.

It didn't stop at that, either. Chrysler was persuaded to supply two Avengers, one for Peter and me and one for Dieter. Robin, meanwhile, was negotiating for a super deluxe team coach for travelling. It was a time of whirlwind activity and we were all greatly impressed. For once it seemed that everyone wanted to get in on the act and help us to our goals.

The first of us to have doubts about this new approach was Willy. The rigorous training methods were aggravating his injured back and he felt he wasn't getting what he needed from Dieter. Because he had had a less successful season than Peter and I his eyes were wide open. We still gave Dieter most of the credit for our results at St Moritz and we could see only good in him – Willy didn't share this view. He saw that the *laissez-faire* comradeship of the Musketeer days was gone, and he was getting no enjoyment from his work. In addition he developed a personality clash with Robin Bailey (another small man) and he felt the time had come to quit. He wanted to continue skiing of course, but he felt he would not be able to do the things he wanted from within the impersonal, big-business organisation that was starting to develop. It was hard for him to leave his friends, and he agonised over the decision for some time. Finally he came to the conclusion that it would be better for him if he continued his own development with the Spanish team, who had offered him use of their facilities.

For me, Willy's departure was a catastrophe. It was the first giant crack in our youthful dreams. I looked to Dieter for help. His attitude was that if Willy spent all his time moaning about his back, we were better off without him. That seemed hard, but my faith in Dieter was still strong and I accepted his view. We hoped to see Willy, of course, as Robin Bailey had told him that if he came back for the team trials in November, and did well, the management would consider meeting his expenses throughout the winter.

There was a long way to go before these trials, however, and we set off to Dachstein to train; it was not a success. I have no doubt that Robin Bailey was genuinely well-intentioned in his desire to broaden the base of British skiing but his new 'mega-squad', though great for the youngsters with stars in their eyes, was not so good for Peter and me. It was a bit like being taken out of a small class in a grammar school and shoved into a comprehensive. Instead of having a trainer to look after our needs exclusively, now we had to share him with a clutch of wide-eyed hopefuls. It was disillusioning. Instead of the young ones being pulled up to our standard we were being dragged down to theirs – at least that's what we felt – and we began to have our doubts about the organisation and about Dieter's training methods.

But it was not yet panic stations. We were still able to talk things over rationally with Dieter and we still valued his skills as a trainer very highly. He had been 'one of us' for too long for us even to consider severing our connection with him. Such a break would have been proof that the old days were dead, and for us that was unthinkable. Besides, his influence on us was still a bit like the Pied Piper, we would still go anywhere with him. It's true we were arguing with him more than we had in the past but we didn't see this as ominous. Dieter was still going to get us to the top – it was our driving force.

While we were braving these embryonic traumas, Willy was quietly working away in the Spanish Pyrenees until the time came for the team trials. These were held at Zauchensee near the Atomic factory and Willy joined us for the week. When he arrived we were doing timed downhills and Willy wiped the floor with us. I was flabbergasted – but not as much as I was when Robin Bailey suggested Peter and I were letting him win so that he qualified for team support.

It was incredible to me that the sport which I had always regarded as clean, honest and wholesome, should now be producing mistrust and innuendo. In effect Robin was saying that I had thrown a fight – something that could not have even entered my head. I was shocked. From that moment on, I never really trusted Robin again.

The first downhill of 1975 was Garmisch Partenkirchen. It was a good course, one that Willy and I both liked, and we wanted to use it as a blow-out before Val d'Isère. Unfortunately for Willy 'blow-out' was to be the right word.

From the moment we arrived, Willy was flying. The little man was using skis five centimetres longer than anyone else (in the cable car to the start his head hardly came up to the bindings, the skis were so big) and he was skiing with enough guts for two men. He was really hungry for success. But God wasn't smiling on Willy at Garmisch. On the second run, pushing it perhaps just a little too hard on his super long skis, Willy crashed at 85mph. It was one of those crashes that television viewers love to watch: skis cartwheeling in the air as they are flung from the boots, arms and legs flailing as the body is bounced and buffeted in a series of horrific collisions with the ground, the sort of crash that appears to break every bone in the skier's body. In fact Willy sat up with little more than concussion; but it was to be his last race.

For me it was a real shame. Of all the Musketeers, Willy probably had the most natural talent (he definitely had a ton of spunk) but he never got the proper direction or help. If he had had his talent properly nurtured, he had the makings of a real winner. He deserved much more than that exit in a shower of snow.

After the crash Willy returned to his home in Switzerland and I jumped into the Avenger for the long drive to the British Championships in Val d'Isère. I did it in eight and a half hours (a time I never bettered until Audi Sport UK lent me a Quattro in my final season) but I arrived only to find that the slalom had already been run. To say I was annoyed would be an understatement. It would have been easy for the officials to delay the race for a day. They knew that Willy and I were expected (they didn't know, of course, about Willy's accident) and they knew that we both wanted to ski the slalom. It was another example of uncaring officialdom and the petty excuses bleated out by Robin Bailey just didn't wash. Okay, so a misunderstanding had occurred, but it was a simple and an honest one – at least that was the officials' viewpoint – and Robin could have been straight about it. He didn't have to be the white-man-speaks-with-forked-tongue of Western fame. Cover-ups only lowered the standing of the sport in the eyes of the press: something that was to come to a head by the time of the Innsbruck Olympics the following year.

Coupled with a growing awareness that the officials were ham-stringing me rather than actively helping was a feeling that Dieter was perhaps not all that he should have been. I had been noticing for some time that we were always skiing better in the summer than in the winter. The other teams were able to build on their summer training when the races of the winter came round. We seemed to be doing the opposite – peaking in the summer and falling off when it really counted. I started to suspect that our training methods were at fault.

Despite these nagging doubts I remained loyal to Dieter until the team for the Innsbruck Olympics was chosen. In a conversation I had had with him about the Olympics he had told me that we would go with a small, compact team; a team with a chance. For me that really meant a team of only four. But when Dieter and Robin Bailey took me aside and told me that it was planned to take a team of six I was floored. The ideal we had worked for, of fielding a British team that was competitive and not a laughing stock, was blown out of the window.

I couldn't believe it. Public money is required to field a team for the Olympics. Now they planned to send people with less of a chance than a snowball in Hell. It was absurd, idiotic, and I was furious. We had made real sacrifices for the sake of British skiing. We were trying to create new standards so that Britain could stand tall with the alpine countries and now it was planned to pad out the group with young boys to ski for their country in the sport's premier competition. These kids had not done the work, and they were aeons from being competitive. For Dieter and Robin to say that it was necessary to give youth a chance was stupid. They had no chance – all they could do was pull the reputation of British skiing, a reputation that we had worked hard to establish, back to square one. Certainly some of those boys had potential – some would almost certainly have their chances in Olympics to come – but this potential should have been carefully nurtured on the FIS European Cup circuit, not at the Olympics where British skiing would be floodlit in the full glare of worldwide television coverage.

But my disaffection with Dieter didn't stop there. In training I had been skiing really well. I had been gliding as fast as Werner Grissman, who was considered the fastest glider on the circuit, and my times were all I could have hoped for. When the time came to start in a FIS downhill at Lienz I was confident and raring to go. Just before the start I spoke to Dieter on the radio to ask him about the state of the course and he told me it was in great condition. With that in mind I pushed myself out of the starting gate and skied fast for the first turn. When I got there I was horrified with what I saw. The course was like the surface of the moon. There were craters and ruts all over the place, the track was in the worst possible condition; it was positively dangerous. I was entering this wasteland at speeds suitable only for a well-prepared course and had no chance when I hit the rubble. I was immediately thrown off balance, caught an edge and disintegrated into a tumbling fall. When I came to a stop I had a searing pain in my knee but that was nothing to the fury I felt inside. What did we pay these trainers for, if not to supply up-to-date and accurate condition reports on the course? For Dieter to have told me the course was good was nothing short of irresponsible: it could have resulted in a fall that took me out of skiing, and in an Olympic year!

When Peter came down the course shortly after me he fell too – not as badly, and he wasn't hurt, but that was due more to luck than to Dieter. When I challenged him about the incident later in the day, he just shrugged it off. It was hard for me to forgive him. When you are working hard towards a goal – in this case Innsbruck – and your trainer puts you into a position that could stop you making it, the result is the evaporation of all trust: and without trust in a trainer there isn't that much hope for a racer.

My knee was agony, I had hurt it several times playing football and I knew I had a bone-spur on the femur that protruded into the muscle, but I refused to believe the fall had caused anything more serious than severe bruising. I wanted desperately to carry on so I treated the knee myself and bound it before heading for Val d'Isère and the next downhill.

When we got there I could hardly bend my leg. I tried skiing the course, which that year was very fast and difficult, but I eventually came to the conclusion that there was no way I was going to make the race. It was a hard decision, but I knew I could not possibly be competitive. When I told Dieter, he reacted with surprise. I told him about the injury, and he countered, in a rather offhand manner, 'I suppose you had better go and have it looked at.'

I was bloody annoyed. I had heard from one of my team-mates that Dieter had been saying I was skiing as badly as he had ever seen. He never came to me to find out if anything was wrong or to discuss what might be done to improve my times. All he could do, it seemed, was mutter to others about the poor performances behind my back. In any other team, even the less well-off ones, a doctor would have been summoned and there would have been considerable concern – especially if it was one of their best hopes who was laid low. Not so with Dieter. He seemed unable to tolerate injury. He had been unsympathetic with Willy's back troubles and he had been less than helpful with Peter's tendon problems. Now he was treating me in the same 'couldn't care less' manner. The two of us were fast moving towards a major confrontation.

That week in Val d'Isère was one of my most miserable in skiing. I was injured, I had had a row with my trainer, and a friend, Michel Dujon, had been killed testing skis at Tignes in preparation for the Val d'Isère race. Michel was France's number one at the time but the reaction of the race organisers, even though they were largely French themselves, was heartless. There was no tribute, no two-minute silence, no nothing. It was business as usual, with the accent on business. It upset me more than I can say. On top of this Ken Read won the actual race, his first win on the World Cup circuit. So there I was, on my way to hospital two months before the Olympics with a friend dead and another winning a race from which I had had to withdraw. The fun of our early days seemed light years in the past.

At hospital in St Anton the doctor told me it would be eight weeks before I could ski again, as my knee had to be opened up. I did my usual trick of dividing whatever a doctor said by two, determining to be on the slopes again within a month to give me a reasonable amount of time to get fit for Innsbruck. Despite being in hospital I was a long way from giving up hope of doing well in the Olympic races.

I was in hospital for a total of nine days. During that time I had one brief 'phone call from Dieter and not a word from the Federation officials in London. It was as though my country had forgotten me. My parents made the effort to come and see me from Kitzbühel but, in the whole of those nine days, they were the only visitors I had. If anything this outward display of neglect on the part of the team management made me even more determined. I wasn't going to let this setback upset my plans. In order to keep in shape I did press-ups in bed and isometric exercises to keep some of the strength in my legs. After constant nagging from me, the doctor let me out of bed on the fourth day, but the pain of the incision was so bad I couldn't get the leg back up onto the bed, and I had to lift it up with my hands. Even so I refused to give up hope and allowed myself no other thoughts than getting better and skiing at Innsbruck.

Two and a half weeks later I was back with the team. My knee was still sore but the first tentative run on skis was reasonably successful and my hopes rose. That afternoon Dieter organised fitness training in the gym. During this session we were asked to play a game of football. I played, conscious of my knee all the time and being very careful, but I couldn't help thinking that it was all a bit stupid. Less than three weeks before I had had a major knee operation yet here I was being asked to play a body contact sport in a fitness programme. The attitude was that, as I was back, I had to do whatever the others did. There was no question of letting me nurse myself back in gently: I had to pull my weight from the word go. Another question-mark lodged in my brain.

The thing about question-marks, of course, is that they evaporate as soon as things start running well. Only four weeks after my operation I entered a European Cup downhill at Haus. My training, despite the still quite delicate knee, had gone well and I was hoping the race would prove to everyone, including myself, that Bartelski was back and hungry.

I needed to build my confidence as this was the last downhill before the Olympics and my only chance to get the problems, including the psychological ones, sorted out.

When the race day came round there was fresh snow on the course which raised my hopes: it was going to suit the gliders. I felt that somebody up there must love me. Ski testing with Blizzard the previous December had sorted the skis out for just this type of course and, although I was determined to do well whatever the condition of the track, I knew that gliding conditions suited me best.

But knowing the conditions would suit me did nothing to calm my nerves. This was a one-off race, the first of the year and, in my own mind (and probably the minds of the Federation), my only pre-Olympics trial. I just had to do well.

In the starting gate all these pressures weighed upon me but once away I had no time to worry: I had to concentrate every second. The thing about soft snow racing is that, although it is essential to get into the best possible low-tucked position, it is also crucial to be as light as possible on the skis. You must let the skis do the work while you steer them with a gentle, almost 'fingertip', control.

At the finish I had no idea how I had done. I wasn't able just to turn round and look at the clock – European Cup races do not have the sophisticated electronic scoreboard equipment that World Cup races have. So, once I had stopped, I had to sweat it out and hope until the time was actually written up on the board. Eventually it went up . . . 1:43.02. I was excited, I knew I was fast, and I began searching the list for faster times. Unfortunately I found one. My friend, Swiss skier Erwin Josi, was just two-hundredths of a second quicker. Elation turned to sickness; to be beaten by less time than it takes to blink an eye is one of the hardest things to take and that so much longed-for win was still eluding me. I was glad, however, for Erwin. If you must be beaten it is better to be beaten by a friend – and Erwin was one of the best.

There were other consolations for me too. Peter Müller – soon to be one of the biggest forces in downhill skiing – could only manage fifth place, while Peter Fuchs and Stuart Fitzsimmons were thirteenth and fourteenth respectively. Three Brits in the top fifteen! This result was brought into even sharper relief when it was realised that both Peter and Stuart skied in ahead of Andy Wenzel and Leonard Stock – skiers who went on to take an overall World Cup and an Olympic gold medal.

At the prize-giving my disappointment was slightly mollified by the sight of the victor's cup. It was a monstrous affair about four feet high – I wouldn't have had anywhere to put it . . . That may have been a silly joke, but it helped make me laugh and enjoy what was undoubtedly a success.

When the excitement was over a throbbing in my knee drew it to my attention. It was red, swollen and obviously in a bad way. Dieter called my surgeon at the hospital in St Anton immediately but, not surprisingly, all the doctor would say was that I was an idiot for skiing on it at all. But despite the pain and the admonition from the doctor I was happy. I had proved my point and I had developed some fragile confidence for Innsbruck. I wasn't carried away, I knew it was just one race, but it was a satisfying way to start the year and a vital boost to my mental preparation.

Innsbruck, compared with Sapporo four years before, was like chalk to cheese. Sapporo had been strange and different, it was a mountain in a country that none of us had seen before, which added to the excitement. Innsbruck, on the other hand, was as familiar as the back garden. In the course of a skiing season we would pass through it perhaps a dozen times; with the Olympics in such a well-known place, we felt that a little gloss had come off the glamour of the event. Originally it had been planned to hold the Olympics in Denver and I couldn't help wishing the plans had not been changed – there is nothing like a strange place and a different culture to supply that little extra charge that good Olympic performances need.

This is not to say that I was unhappy about Innsbruck. Well-known ground was neither an advantage nor a disadvantage: it was going to be the same for all the racers and I, for one, was happy just to be there.

There were differences, of course. Innsbruck for the Olympics was nothing like Innsbruck for a FIS race. On entering the town in our team Avenger, Stuart Fitzsimmons and I were stopped at a check-point. We had to prove our bona fides and get identity and security passes before being allowed into the village itself. Once there Peter Fuchs and I settled into a small apartment – again as different from Sapporo as it is possible to imagine. In Innsbruck the beds were as hard as concrete. The first time I threw myself onto mine I nearly broke my back. Unfortunately the course proved to be no better.

Despite knowing the hills of Innsbruck well I was keen to see the Olympic run. It is always necessary, if you are to go over and over the race in your mind, to be able to picture it exactly as you will find it on the race proper.

What I found was a nightmare. From top to bottom the course was lightning fast, boiler-plate ice; little short of being suicidally dangerous. When they realised how difficult the course was the organisers changed the track slightly, but it was still an extremely difficult downhill indeed. Conditions were not made any better by the fact that the surface was melted with heated reflectors during the day and allowed to freeze into a smooth sheet of ice at night. The racing conditions were the very opposite of the soft snow, gliding conditions I had found at Haus.

In our own camp Dieter was becoming fanatical about ski preparation. If he found just a speck of dust in the ski-room the air would go blue as he yelled abuse at whoever was responsible. As the bob-sleigh people shared the same facilities, and as they were spraying down their machines, this didn't make for a peaceful time.

On the slope itself I wasn't having a very happy time either. The icy course was so quick that I had to struggle just to keep within the flags but, after one run, I noticed that the edges of my skis were blunt. I brought this to the attention of Dieter, a man who seemed to be thinking of nothing else but ski care, and his reply was that I always seemed to go faster on blunt edges. That was stupidity beyond belief. I checked the Swiss and Austrian skis and almost cut my fingers on their razor-sharp edges. It made me furious. There were only three days of practice at the Olympics and to waste one of them because of blunt skis was ridiculous.

The result of all this was that the atmosphere in the camp was very low. We were all – and perhaps me in particular – struggling to find form, yet all around us, at least so it seemed, was discord and acrimony. Our manager, Robin Bailey, was having battles with the press, too. They didn't seem to be on our side as they had been in the past.

Later, when Robin Bailey left the team, our hassles with the press seemed to dissolve, which I don't think was a coincidence. Robin seemed to have a way of getting people's backs up and he had no idea of how to deal with journalists. Most of those who covered our activities were experienced; hard-bitten hacks who could see through Robin's excuses and evasions as easily as they could down a pint of beer. They wanted the truth about the team, pure and simple. From Robin they never got it and the animosity that built up between him and the press corps carried over into the team and dampened our spirits.

The effect was that my own confidence was partially eroded. Bickering and outright argument had taken its toll and I was a bundle of nerves when I got to the start-gate for the race. Even so I forced myself to concentrate. I talked to myself out loud. 'You can do it . . . you can do it', I said over and over as I approached the start-hut. Indeed, my concentration was so intense that only the wild euphoria that greeted the brilliant winning run of Franz Klammer could shake me, and even then only momentarily, from it. I was as keen as I had ever been to get my head down, take the risks and do my very best for Britain.

But I made an idiotic mistake. For the first quarter or so of the course I was skiing well – only about a second down on Klammer's time – but I got myself too far back on my skis in a compression and fell. It was a stupid fall and I was furious with myself, but it was the type of fall that I am sure I would never have made had things been going right off the track. It was the fall of a skier who lacked a really positive approach and I was angry with myself for letting the team-room rows get me down so much.

It was, to me at least, the familiar sad and introspective Bartelski who trudged a lonely path away from the finish area. Pondering my future had become almost a post-race habit. The crowds were pouring off the hill buzzing with excitement at Klammer's win and taking very little notice of me. I was not completely ignored: some children stopped me and asked for my autograph and, as I obliged, I noticed two of the prettiest girls about fifty yards away. To hell with the lost race, these two ladies became my new target. I knew they had been looking at me but I was too shy (in spite of a reputation as a womaniser, somewhat exaggerated, I was not a fast worker) to approach them direct, so I started to follow them. For a while I lost them but, from a bus, I saw them again and beckoned them over. It turned out they were Americans and I invited them to a party we were planning to hold that night. Alas they could not come as they were travelling to Zurich that night. Another near-miss for Bartelski.

Before parting I got their names and addresses saying, as one does, that if ever I was in America I would drop in. I did more than that. The following year I flew to the States, took a three-thousand-mile Greyhound bus trip and visited them both. We had a wonderful time and the three of us are still great friends. They were by far the best thing that happened to me on that otherwise totally miserable Innsbruck day.

THE BRICK WALL

*   *   *

Post-Olympic years are always lean. There is no money left in the kitty and the team runs on a shoestring for a while. I had anticipated this but I never thought of giving up racing. Some of the journalists, particularly John Hennessy, had speculated that I might be on the verge of retirement. Such a thought had never crossed my mind. How could it? Innsbruck was a setback, certainly, but I had had them before. If those Olympics were deleted my record showed that I was on the up and up. I still had great dreams and, despite the financial disadvantages of being a British skier, my main desire was to go on skiing for my country until those dreams were realised.

But for that to happen things had to change. If we were going to do things on a low budget we had to lower our costs without lowering efficiency: indeed we had to increase efficiency despite the lack of cash. Peter and I began to occupy ourselves in thinking of ways this might be done.

The coaching system was the first thing to come under our scrutiny. We felt that an obvious reform would be for Dieter to train the men's and the women's teams together. If these squads were small, just the men and women with the most potential, it would cut the costs, solve the problems of logistics and allow us to train together. This would give the women the incentive of getting closer to the higher standards set by the men and would establish a tight nucleus that had a chance in the cut-throat competition of the 'white circus'.

The first opportunity we had to air our views was at the Colyum Bridge Hotel, near Cairngorm, at the time of the British Championships in April 1976. We were all housebound at the time as the wind was blowing so hard up the mountain that we would have gone uphill rather than down had we tried to ski. I decided this was a heaven-sent opportunity and suggested to George Stewart, the chairman of the Federation's Alpine Committee, that we hold a meeting there and then. This was to include the press and the sponsors as well as the teams, and was to be a total and complete airing of the problems facing British skiing. I had always felt there should be no secrets in the sport and, after the bad press following the Olympics, I felt the time had come to heal the rift and create an atmosphere conducive to mutual understanding.

George Stewart agreed readily and twenty minutes later we were crowded into the hotel ballroom for the meeting.

Most of the talking was done by me for the men and Fiona Easdale for the women. We were trying to get some form of commitment from the Federation for the following year but we seemed to be bashing our heads against a brick wall. No matter how hard we tried we could not get the sport's controllers to commit themselves to anything tangible as far as the future went. It made me very cross because the kids in the sport had already made a not inconsiderable commitment. They had given up a lot to go ski racing and we felt it was up to the Federation to give them the backing and security that was their due. But it was no good. The Federation, we were told, was financially embarrassed and no hard-and-fast promises could be made. John Samuel, of *The Guardian*, who was sitting in on the meeting, made a speech that summed things up perfectly. John called on everyone to accept their responsibilities and pointed out to the Federation the urgency of coming up with detailed and structured plans, both for the skiers themselves and the future of the sport. Still George Stewart and his committee members did not budge. George was employed by the Forestry Commission at the time and Stuart Fitzsimmons, at his most perceptive, said to me at the end of the almost four-hour meeting: 'Now I know why trees grow so slow!'

On the coaching front, the plan that Peter and I had devised was accepted. There was no argument to its logic and it was decided to put it into effect immediately. For this plan we remained loyal to Dieter. We thought that the extra responsibility and authority would give him confidence to work as constructively as we had done in the Musketeer days. It is worth mentioning here that I regarded Dieter as my friend and, despite the differences of opinion we had been having, I was unable even to think of asking for him to be replaced. I was loyal to him and I felt he was basically loyal to me: a year later things would be very different indeed.

The first decision that Dieter made in his new expanded role was that I should go to Argentina for a FIS downhill with the Americans and Canadians. He felt that this would help me consolidate my good result at Haus as well as giving me the opportunity to take part in a really competitive downhill during the lull of the northern summer season. All the arrangements were made and, during the last week before departure, I spent fourteen hours a day with Dieter building the basement of his house near Zell am See. I didn't regret giving him this time – indeed, we had been so close that, had the positions been reversed and it was me building a house, I would have half expected him to do the same for me.

Peter wasn't going to Argentina because, finally, a doctor had been found who could do something about his Achilles tendon. He was to go into hospital at Farnham in Surrey and was expected to be out of action until October.

Thanks again to the cheap travel I could arrange through my father, I found myself on a KLM DC8 to Buenos Aires. I had no briefing and was travelling virtually blind into what can only be described as the unknown. All I knew was that I had to land at Buenos Aires and find an internal flight to Bariloche. When I arrived I was to contact the local Bariloche Ski Club and put myself in their hands.

At Buenos Aires airport I saw a couple of other ski bags coming down the ramp that were not mine and, looking around, I found myself standing next to Ron Fuller, an American against whom I had raced occasionally in Europe. Ron was in Argentina to take a ski-camp for American youngsters and they also were going to Bariloche.

Naturally I asked if I could share their transport to the resort and they were only too happy to oblige; indeed they did more than that, inviting me to join them and train with them in their camp. It was perfect for me to have keen, English-speaking racers to train with, while the youngsters of the American squad were thrilled to have someone from a national squad training with them.

Once in Bariloche I settled into the strict discipline of their camp and found out, perhaps for the first time in my life, what real training was all about. These guys were actually being *trained*. They were not just going down the mountain trying, every time, to be faster than they had been the last time. They worked on technique and balance as well as speed – it was a real eye-opener. I completely immersed myself in their training, and I felt uplifted and happy. My buoyancy was a combination of everything: the beautiful landscape and birds (to ski on a wild, open mountain with a twelve-foot wingspan condor soaring over my head was a thrill I will never forget), the friendliness of the people, the glorious (and cheap) food and the good comradeship of those young Americans. It was just what I needed.

When the race came round I felt I had a real chance. I had trained well and I was fairly confident: but I bombed it. A third of the way down the course I took one risk too many and came to grief. It wasn't a dangerous fall and I wasn't injured – but I was out of the race, and I would have no result to take back to England. Naturally I was a little disappointed, but not unduly so: so I had bombed out, it wasn't the first time and it wouldn't be the last. Ski racing requires a fine line and if you step off it you are done for. I had tried too hard and paid the penalty. It was a hazard of the job.

After the race I decided to stay on another fortnight with the Americans. I was getting real benefit from their camp and it seemed stupid not to take advantage of it – especially as Argentina had better snow and conditions than any European summer ski area. The chance they offered me was not to be missed; and there was the added bonus that the Canadian national team were there as well.

When the time finally came to leave I had only one regret. Despite all the hard training I had put on eight pounds in weight. All that wonderful cheap food had gone to my head (and my stomach) and I had eaten as much in a month as some people would eat in a year. I knew it had to come off but I can't say I regretted a minute of the time spent putting it on.

Back in Europe, the first thing I did was to visit Dieter, who was training with the team at Hintertux. I was full of my trip and I wanted to tell my friends about it but I was greeted by a group of people who seemed to have had their vitality surgically removed. The atmosphere was a stark contrast to the enthusiasm and *joie de vivre* I had left behind in Argentina. Dieter treated my arrival with a noticeable lack of enthusiasm. I wanted to sit down and regale him with the events of my trip but, despite my obvious jet lag, he reacted as though I had never been away. I was included in a training game of football but the atmosphere was so disheartening that I left within two hours to go home to my parents. The only enjoyment I had that day was the exhilaration of the drive over the twists and turns of the Gerlos Pass on my way to my parents' new house – only a hundred yards across the fields from Dieter's!

One week on a carrot-juice diet coupled with cycle rides up the Gross Glockner road and I had shed my surplus eight pounds. I was now at skiing weight again and rejoined the team in training at Obertraun.

The first training session took place in the gym, doing circuits of a minute and a half duration. This means doing a minute and a half of press-ups followed by a minute and a half of sit-ups, and so on. It is very exhausting work and it seemed strange to me that Dieter was demanding it – three years before he had told me that it was unwise for skiers to do these exercises for more than one-minute spells. Even more than that, I was surprised that Dieter should require this sort of work from the team so late in the season; it was September and if they hadn't got past the need for pure strength training there was no hope for them.

When the session was over I went up to Dieter and reminded him of his earlier statement. His reply was brief and to the point. '– – – – – – off.'

It was like a slap in the face and I was hurt. In the past, we had been friends and colleagues who discussed things between ourselves and came to collective decisions. Now he was the boss and it had gone to his head. He couldn't tolerate me questioning his decisions and we had a mammoth row there and then on the tennis court. At the end of it I had no one to turn to so I rang my parents – if only to speak with somebody sane.

Peter was recuperating from his operation in Scotland, Willy was in Switzerland, and now Dieter had turned against me. I was on my own. Exit the Three Musketeers, enter the Lone Ranger.

I persevered with that week's training but the atmosphere was taut to say the least. If Dieter demanded a form of training that didn't make sense to me I wouldn't do it. I spoke with other people on the team to see if they felt as I did. Most of them had reservations about Dieter's methods – the only difference being that they wouldn't voice them. I wasn't exactly alone but I had no visible allies. With a mixture of concern for the future and relief to be leaving, I left Obertraun at the end of the week. My only thought was to get to Scotland to confer with Peter; he was the only person with whom I could still communicate.

The welcome that I received at the Fuchs home in Carrbridge was another vivid contrast to the lack of enthusiasm at Obertraun. It was really good to be back with a family who were happy and who understood the problems I was experiencing. Peter and I spent a few days together discussing the deterioration in team morale – he was in complete sympathy with me – but mainly we tried to relax and have a little fun. We knew when we rejoined the team at Meadowbank for fitness training there would be friction and we wanted to have as friction-free a time as possible until then.

We drove down to the training in Peter's new Lotus 7 but about sixty miles north of Perth on the A9 a sheep jumped out in front of us in the rain. We swerved to avoid it but, in doing so, slid off the road, hit a rock and put a hole in the sump. All we could do was arrange a tow to a local garage where we talked an unco-operative garageman into welding the hole. He agreed only if we removed the sump and did the refitting ourselves. We had no choice. Knowing that we would be late for training, we tried to ring the hotel where we were booked to leave a message but were unable to get through. When we eventually got to Meadowbank we were three hours late.

As we walked into the room where the team were, Dieter looked up and said, sarcastically: 'Here come the two Sirs.' It didn't bother me. By now I was becoming inured to Dieter's barbs; but I thought it unforgivable that Dieter should adopt this approach with Peter. The two of them hadn't seen each other for several months. In that time Peter had undergone a serious tendon operation that required a long period of recuperation. Under such circumstances I would have expected Dieter to welcome Peter cordially and perhaps have a look to see what sort of job the surgeon had done. Not a bit of it. Peter was with me, and I was the black sheep – so he got the same treatment. This attitude was another major blow to whatever lingering respect I still had for our coach, making working conditions between us very difficult indeed. I found his behaviour rude and unpardonable.

Difficult or not, we still had to knuckle down and train, and we did just that. Things were just as unpleasant as we had envisaged and I felt obliged to telephone Ian Graeme, general secretary of the Federation in London, to put him in the picture. I told him of the very low morale, indicated some of the problems with Dieter, and suggested that the Federation would do well to keep an eye on things.

I got the usual bureaucratic, non-committal response. Instead of being concerned about the sorry situation I was revealing – a situation, in effect of stagnation – I was told not to worry, that things couldn't be that bad and that I should try to get on with the training. Obviously the urgency that I felt, the urgency that had prompted me to make the call, wasn't getting through. More than ever, I felt in a position of isolation.

From now on training was punctuated by slanging matches and arguments. It was no fun being in the squad and I was doing it only as work – all the pleasure that had motivated my skiing in the Musketeer days, and with the American lads at Bariloche, was now well in the past. Training had become an unpleasant chore.

At Montgenevre at the end of November, in training for a FIS downhill, all the bickering and tension within the camp seemed to come to a head within me and mentally I was ill-equipped to race. Almost inevitably I crashed in training. It was a heavy, spinning, fall and I literally saw stars. There was no possibility of continuing with training that day and I spent the rest of it on the bed in my hotel room. It was a miserable start to the season, which continued in Val Gardena where I hurt myself again. I was not a happy man.

While I was off hurt, however, I travelled to Zell am See to help Dieter with the girls' team. We seemed to work quite well together and things were looking a little more hopeful when training stopped for Christmas.

The conviviality of Christmas had always been a tonic to me and a time when I could relax, but this time I knew I had to use the lay-off to come to terms with the current problems. I knew I had become too introverted and serious and I had to find a way out of it. Dieter and his wife, Judy, were close friends of my family and lived within view of my parents' house. Christmas provided an opportunity for us to get together to see if we could patch up our differences and recreate the sort of constructive working conditions that could lead to positive results.

We had several discussions together over that holiday period and I was heartened by the thought that we were getting somewhere. Within the tranquillity of our homes the animosity inherent in our coach/racer relationship disappeared. We became friends again and Dieter was prepared to listen to my views. For those few weeks I thought that the storm, at last, was over: in fact it had only just begun.

After Christmas I spent a few days with the Canadian team, who were training at Flums in Switzerland. Their good humour – boisterous good humour at times – coupled with a positive sense of purpose served only to make me more depressed. Everything they had was lacking in our camp. I felt jealous of their spirit and conviction and my hotel room became like a prison cell. I could see no way out of the dead-end that the British team had blundered into.

The first race in January 1977 was at Garmisch and I arrived for it only to find that Dieter wasn't there. He had gone off with the girls' team and had left his assistant, Koni Rupprechter, in charge.

I was livid. One of the things Dieter and I had agreed over Christmas was that he should be there for the race. Now I found myself with a trainer who, although nice enough, had little experience at that time of World Cup downhill and who certainly wasn't the answer to the mess the team was in.

Training went poorly and the strain was building up inexorably within me. A friendship I had with a girl racer on the German team, Monika Bader, broke up and it was the last straw. On a training run that evening I collapsed. I cried uncontrollably for two hours and was as forlorn and disconsolate as I had ever been. I had broken down completely.

But there was a race the next day and at the start I summoned all my inner resources to build up a fierce determination. I went at the course like a man possessed, hell-bent on giving my best, but coming into a long, fast, 85mph-turn (appropriately named *Holle* – German for Hell), I ran out of steam. I felt completely drained of energy. With only dregs of strength left I managed narrowly to avoid hitting the trees and struggled to the finish totally exhausted. For the first two-thirds of the course I had been among the top twenty and skiing well, but the 'wall' I hit at Holle cost me three full seconds and put me right out of the picture.

I was absolutely shattered. So much so that I poured my heart out to *Guardian* sports editor John Samuel. All my misgivings about team management came tumbling out. The lack of morale, the coaching problems – and particularly my conviction that Koni simply lacked the experience to do the job – and my own frustrations were all revealed in a long interview. The result was a piece in *The Guardian* the next day airing some of my misgivings and anxieties for the first time. It caused the waves to whip up a little higher and the coming storm was that much closer.

After that race Koni wanted me to join the team for a Europa Cup race somewhere in France but I, almost masochistically, insisted on going on to Kitzbühel for the Hahnenkamm. After such appalling results, and my near-nervous breakdown, tackling the toughest downhill on the circuit was a bit pie-in-the-sky. But I had to get away: I had to be away from the team for a while. So it was against team orders that I travelled to Kitzbühel and joined up with my friends on the Canadian team.

The sparks soon turned into flames: I was threatened with two weeks suspension by the Federation.

My parents came to visit me and, frankly, were appalled. They had seen me nearly killed on television two years before and now they saw me as a shadow of my former self, skiing under almost unbearable strain. They were actually scared for me and said so.

After many heated 'phone conversations with Dieter, the threat of suspension was lifted and a compromise was reached. I would race at Kitzbühel and rejoin the team the following week provided that Sigi Bernegger, the ex-Austrian coach, came along to give the team the benefit of his downhill experience.

Kitzbühel was a disaster. I was way off the pace and was 'out to lunch'. I just wasn't with it. But in the next race, a Europa Cup downhill at San Sicario under Sigi's guidance, I was tenth.

During the coaching troubles with Dieter and Koni I had begun to wonder whether the problem was in me. I had become self-analytical to such an extent that I couldn't see the wood for the trees. Under Sigi things were different. He had authority and vast experience. He demanded discipline, of course, but I bowed to it readily out of sheer respect for the man's ability. Under him I began to rebuild my own self-respect and confidence and to get a real kick out of my skiing again.

My spirits had been lifted, too, by Dieter saying that I could go to Lake Louise in Canada for the Canadian Championships. I was really excited by the prospect of racing in such a stimulating environment. I had arranged my tickets and things were all set but, at a FIS race in Austria, Dieter changed his mind and said I couldn't go.

I lost my cool completely. All the anger and frustration came out in a torrent of shouting and cursing. I couldn't understand why we had to be subjected to this sort of crap, and I told him so. The row shattered the last vestiges of loyalty I had for him.

The next few races were a joke. It was impossible to operate properly under such strained circumstances and, although I tried my best, I could do no better than twenty-sixth at a downhill in Laax. During this period my father, out of concern for my safety (and even my mental health) had gone to Dieter's house in an attempt to sort things out. Dieter was unmoved. As far as he was concerned there would be no problems so long as I knuckled down under his authority and accepted all his decisions. He said that I was a maverick, scornful of his position in the team, and implied that all the blame for the breakdown in our relationship was mine. My father reminded him of the way he had mishandled Willy and the indifference he had shown to Peter and me when we had been getting over fairly serious injuries. It was quite a slanging match.

The importance of this episode in the story stems from the fact that my father had always tried to keep his involvement in my skiing just to being a supporter. It was my life and I was doing my thing. He left me alone to get on with it and I appreciated that. The fact that my father felt he had to step in indicates the extent to which things had deteriorated.

Knowing that I was unlikely to get anywhere talking to Dieter, my next step was to write to the Federation. It was a strong letter, but it put the case as I saw it rationally. I explained the breakdown in trust and the serious problems with morale and I said that I hoped my letter would lead to a meeting where we could all sit down as sensible human beings and sort things out. In order not to be thought to be doing anything behind Dieter's back, I sent a copy of the letter to him too.

During training over the following few weeks there was no response from the Federation but the reaction of the trainers, both Dieter and Koni, was clear and unequivocal. I had been sent to Coventry.

It was a totally untenable position. My parents stepped in again in an attempt to clear the air. Because my father felt he was too biased, following his row with Dieter, my mother travelled to London to talk to Federation Secretary Major-General Graeme. It was not a successful meeting. Without ceremony and in a manner verging on rudeness, Major-General Graeme told my mother what a bad boy I was. He suggested that the reason I had done poorly in South America was because I spent all my time womanising and that I was a bad influence on the team. My mother was unable to get any hearing for my own case and she returned home to Zell am See visibly shocked.

To me it was incredible. There I was trying to pursue my sport and get British skiing respected in the world, and all I got was a kick in the face from my own Federation. Even worse, some sections of the Federation treated my parents with contempt as well. It was appalling.

The next major development was a meeting between the team, Dieter, and General Graeme, at the European Cup Finals in Italy. Although I was not actually in Coventry now, Dieter was distinctly cold towards me and the atmosphere was unpleasant.

General Graeme started to outline the plans for the team for the coming year and it was as though all the things I had said, all the problems I had brought to his attention, had fallen on deaf ears. Along with some of the others I again put the case for change, for the positive encouragement of excellence, but still General Graeme and Dieter refused to be moved. It is interesting to note here that several of the team members who had expressed similar views to mine during private discussions kept silent during the meeting. To General Graeme it must have seemed as though I was acting alone, which would have reinforced his view that I was the stirrer in the squad.

As the Federation's plans for the next year began to unfold I became more and more convinced that there was no hope. It was the old, old line that practical experience on the race courses had proven to be wrong. All the old frustrations began to build up again and I started to get sharp, stabbing, headaches behind my left eye – headaches that got progressively worse over the ensuing weeks.

As the pains increased in intensity I began to worry. I had had a bad fall at Montgenevre not long before and I knew that, in order to be on the safe side, it was necessary to see a neurologist. An appointment was made with a London specialist as soon as possible after the Scottish Championships, which were held at Cairngorm on 17 and 18 April, 1977.

During this time I was summoned to meet a special committee of three Federation officials so that I could put my side of the story. The meeting was to take place on 22 April; the same day I was to see the neurologist.

The Scottish Championships were important to me. I wanted to show everyone that I could still win. Peter, after having had a bad season with minor complications following his operation, pipped me in the giant slalom but I won the slalom, and took the overall championship ahead of Alan Stewart. It was an almost uncanny coincidence that this was the same result we had had at the start of our time as the Three Musketeers: another full circle turned.

At the meeting I put my case as fairly as I could. It was a long session (it had to be adjourned in the afternoon while I saw the neurologist) and I went through the events of the year as dispassionately as I could. I reiterated my view that it was unfair to ask young skiers to train under a coach for whom 'yes' did not mean 'yes' and 'no' did not mean 'no', and I pointed out how difficult it would be, if not impossible, to continue working under a man for whom I now had no respect.

The committee listened attentively and several options were discussed to get over the problem. One was that I leave the team but continue to ski under a British licence. This would have meant that I could make my own arrangements for training but continue to ski for Britain in races. It seemed quite a sensible solution for me personally but did little for the younger skiers, skiers to whom Britain was looking for the future, who would have to continue working in an obsolete and impracticable way.

I put my case so strongly that I felt if anybody could go along with Dieter after it they just could not have been listening.

The following day I was summoned again. This time I was to see Alan Stewart's father, George Stewart, chairman of the Federation's Alpine Committee.

THE BRICK WALL

I sat down, to hear the father of a team member I had beaten just a few days before tell me that I was no longer on that team and that I was no longer allowed to represent my òwn country.

The next day I woke up without a pain in my head!

— 5 —
BRIDGING THE
GAP

I was on the dole. Unfairly dismissed without doubt but I had no union to plead my case. Even if I had had one it is unlikely that much could have been done; my former employers were so powerful and safe in the armchairs of their ivory tower that they didn't even feel the need to make a public statement about my dismissal. As in George Orwell's *1984*, I had not just ceased to exist, I had never existed. The silence of the Federation fairly shouted their belief that my expulsion was such an insignificant and trifling matter that explanation was unnecessary.

In order to give my plight some wider airing I rang John Samuel and a lengthy piece appeared in *The Guardian* the next day under the banner 'Bartelski dropped'. In it John reprinted part of a letter from General Graeme which came following my demand to have the dismissal in writing.

The letter said:

'You made it very clear to me that you were not prepared to be a co-operative member of the British team. In making plans for the 1977–78 season Dieter Bartsch and I have agreed that you should not be a member of the British Alpine team.'

The letter went on to say that I was also to be denied a licence to race as a Briton.

When John Samuel put this to Ian Graeme later, the General said: 'Konrad was not prepared to be a team member in the way we think necessary. He wanted too many of the resources for himself. We cannot issue him with a start licence in case he turns up at a World Cup race and takes one of the British quota which we want for a team member.'

So, in one fell swoop, they not only took away my livelihood by giving me the sack, they also banned me from getting a job in my own country.

It is ironic that most of the people who control skiing in this country are also people who have never been anywhere near a World Cup race. They are, of course, assumed to have such knowledge by those outside the sport (and, sadly, by some within) and this has put them into positions so lofty that no mere layman – and to some people on the committees virtually everyone other than their own number is a layman – is qualified to question any of their decisions.

In this case I was sacked for attitudes sincerely held, about aspects of World Cup, our organisation and training methods, by people who apparently had only the sketchiest idea of what I was talking about. Admittedly there may have been times when I put my case badly, or expressed myself too forcefully: but then I wasn't a politician, I was a skier. Success was always my aim, and I just didn't feel that everyone was on the same side.

From now on the administrators would have even less idea of what I was talking about as, in order to carry on skiing, I had to brush up my Dutch! Following a letter of request, and with the help of Tom van de Meer who was striving to reorganise the Dutch team, I turned traitor. I painted out the Union Jack on my helmet and replaced it with the red, white and blue stripes of the Netherlands. The Dutch had made me an official member of their team and they gave me the use of their coaches and training facilities. There was, however, to be no financial support and somehow I had to get myself special downhill coaching as the Dutch did not train their skiers in that discipline.

So my first problem was cash. Despite being determined to ski on I was forced to live from day to day until I managed to arrange sponsorship from Salomon of about £2,500. That was a big help but I knew I would have to develop my penny-pinching techniques; techniques that I had fortunately learned from one of the world's greatest masters – Peter Fuchs.

During this period Peter was skiing with the British team but the scar from his tendon operation, which was still tender, made it virtually impossible for him to be at all comfortable in his boots. He was still skiing well – his win in the Scottish Championships giant slalom was ample testimony to that – but he was thoroughly disheartened. So much so that, after my expulsion, Peter wrote a letter in support of me to the Federation and refused to continue to train under Dieter. He asked the Federation for an independent start licence (the type of licence I had already been refused) and was given until 2 November to explain his reasons. He was also required to supply details of his fitness and the schedule of his summer training. This was too much for Peter. In desperation he made the decision not to race outside Scotland. As he said to me later: 'I am just fed up with the whole thing.'

So, as well as sacking me, the Federation effectively sacked Peter too. They never actually showed him the door, but they made things so awkward that he felt he had little choice.

The Alpine Committee must have been thoroughly pleased with themselves. Both their prime dissenters were in the wilderness, everything in their garden was peaceful and quiet again, and they could enjoy their gins-and-tonics without the disruption of either Bartelski or Fuchs. That they had lost the two best skiers on the squad didn't seem to bother them a bit.

Despite the Dutch flag on my hat, I hadn't changed: my nationality hadn't changed, my passport hadn't changed, and my loyalties hadn't changed. As far as I was concerned I was a British skier. The only difference between now and before was that I wanted to beat the people who made up the official British team even more than ever.

The task for me now was to put into practice the ideas I had fought for in the British team. Most of the training disagreements had been over physical training and I started to train by my own ideas, in my own way. Instead of doing every type of work, whether I enjoyed it or not, I concentrated on the aspects of training that I actually enjoyed, my belief being that training that is fun is automatically better training. I also did nothing to overtax my body. Instead of training till I dropped from sheer exhaustion, and as a result feeling stiff and sluggish the next day, I paced myself to get maximum benefit from the exercises.

For actual ski training I went, once again, to Bariloche in Argentina. I was unable to afford to stay with the Americans, who were again in their camp. Instead I rented, very cheaply, a room in a private house. It was one of the most sinister-looking places I have ever seen. The house was surrounded by a huge fifteen-foot high wall and the owner, a German who slept with a gun under his bed and a savage Alsatian dog on hand, insisted that if I brought round a visitor it must, under no circumstances, be a local. He refused to allow anyone who lived in Bariloche to see inside his house!

Low-cost though my board and lodging was, living in Bariloche was no longer cheap. Argentina's hundred per cent inflation rate had taken its toll and I was forced to sell a couple of pairs of skis in order to be able to make ends meet. Even so I was able to train with the Swiss whose national squad was down for summer training. All the guys on the Swiss team, Bernard Russi, Erwin Josi and Martin Berthod in particular, were friends of long standing and it was a real pleasure for me to train with them.

That training taught me a lot, but the best part of the trip came when I met up with the Swiss boys in Rio on the way home. Rio is a swinging town twelve months of the year and the gaiety and sunshine went to our heads very quickly. At last I was enjoying life again. The internecine strife and the depressions of the battle with the British authorities were easily forgotten in that wonderful city. Whether I was lazing on Copacabana beach looking at the girls or just generally chatting in an open air bar, this was a time of carefree battery-charging for me. Good company and that glorious city were a better tonic than any a doctor could have prescribed.

Back in Europe Karl Kahr, the coach of the Austrian team, allowed me to train on their downhill course at Hintertux. Karl had at one stage been trainer of the British women's team and he knew something of what I had been up against. He did not require any persuading to let me train with his team and the opportunity to do so was just what I needed.

I took a cheap bed-and-breakfast room as a second home and got down to very intensive training. Over about two and a half months I put in more miles of downhill training than I had ever done before. Nobody was actually coaching me and I didn't have the advantage of video but I felt I got a great deal out of the training and the mileage had me popping out of my skin with race-fitness.

The first races of the season were a World series at Crans Montana. These were pre-World Cup openers and I knew that, if I was to give my best, I would need someone to give me pointers during the practices. Who better than Peter Fuchs?

Peter and his girlfriend had travelled to Crans with me and he was only too happy to act as my coach. For my part I was delighted to have someone who knew my skiing as well as Peter did to assist with my training.

Peter and I were effectively a British team; but we would be doing battle with the official British team when the races came. Even so, although I wanted to beat them, my objective was to beat the Austrians – they presented the real challenge.

Throughout the training in Crans I had perpetual problems with my skis. I was skiing on Blizzard and, as I was now skiing alone, had asked the company for the use of their technician to prepare my skis for the races. Blizzard agreed readily enough but the technician treated my skis very much as second cousins. They were never properly scraped down after practice and the general maintenance left much to be desired. The experience convinced me that I would have to switch ski manufacturers.

Despite these problems, however, the race result was not too bad for me. I was twenty-fourth and on the right track. That encouraged me, and I looked forward to the first World Cup race at Val d'Isère with relish.

Before Val d'Isère there was a small Europa Cup race at Tignes and I took the opportunity to approach Rossignol about skis. They agreed to supply me with skis and service but they could offer me no financial support. The skis were to be looked after by the Swiss team technician but, for the Val d'Isère race, were to be serviced by the Canadian man. Unfortunately he got them all wrong. I finished sixty-first, behind even Stuart Fitzsimmons and David Cargill of the British team, but I knew the problem was all in the skis. My opinion was borne out by the fact that a Canadian on similarly-prepared skis, who came down ten minutes after me, could hardly get to the end of the flats the skis were running so badly. It was a wasted chance and I was upset but I knew it was a problem that could be sorted out with more skilful preparation.

Peter was with me in Val d'Isère and he was a great help, spiritually as well as technically, but unfortunately he was unable to stay for any more races. He promised to join up with me again for the all-important World Championships at Garmisch later in the season but, until then, I was to be alone. It wasn't a pleasant prospect and

I didn't look forward to the long drive to the next race at Val Gardena. However, I had been seeing something of an American girl in Val d'Isère, and I asked her if she would like to come for a week's skiing in Italy. I thought she would make a pleasant change to the car cassettes which I now knew by heart . . .

The following morning she was waiting outside her hotel and together we set off for the long drive. Everything went well until we got to the Swiss border – she hadn't got a passport. The Swiss border guards, and the Austrian ones when we got that far, proved reasonable. Upon proof of her identity they let her through provided it was just for transit. At the Italian border things were not so easy.

The Italian guards were not impressed by her identification papers and refused her entry. I was in a quandary. I didn't know whether to send her all the way back or what. In the end I decided to take a risk. I took my gear out of the boot, packed her in the bottom and put the cases back on top of her. We then went through customs at another checkpoint. What would have happened if they had discovered her I will never know – nothing very pleasant I am sure – but the ruse was successful. As a skier I was still alone, but at least I had a companion for a week.

Being a loner on the circuit had its good and bad aspects. It was good to be able to finish skiing at the end of the day and not have to talk about skiing all the time. It was also stimulating facing the challenge of having to make it alone in a dog-eat-dog sport. On the other hand, when I stood at the top ten minutes before the start and looked at the physios, masseurs, expensive electronic communication systems and the like sported by the big teams, I couldn't help wondering what the hell I was doing. I felt a little like a go-kart on a Grand Prix grid: a minnow amongst whales.

I had to find a way of overcoming these feelings if I was to be able to do myself justice, so I bought myself what was in those days the equivalent of a Sony Walkman and spent the last twenty minutes or so before a race listening to the Little Feat album *Time Loves a Hero*. This simple idea solved many of my problems. The music drowned out the distracting race talk of the other teams and gave me the opportunity to go over the race in my own mind in peace. I would sit alone with my headphones on, getting charged by the music and preparing for the race all at the same time.

Using this technique I found that, when race time came, I was still hyped up by the music. My mind was free of extraneous thoughts and my body straining at the leash to go.

Some time after this I met the drummer of Little Feat, Richie Hayward, and told him how important his music had been to me. He was amazed by the bizarre use to which the music was being put, while at the same time, of course, he was flattered!

The Val Gardena race went like a dream. I literally skimmed over the course, I felt I was going so fast I was hardly in touch with the snow. I was sixteenth – still six places off a World Cup point, but it was the best-ever 'British' men's World Cup result. And I had done it alone – the 'official' British were floundering in my wake.

To a large extent I had proved my point and the pressure was off. The training methods I had been advocating for the British team had worked for me.

From Val Gardena until the World Championships in February my results, although not spectacular, were consistently better than anything I had done in the past. I was really beginning to knock on the door but a pattern was emerging. I found that I tended to be a little slow on the first part of the course only to pick up speed towards the finish. This was gratifying from the fitness point of view – it was another indication that my training methods were efficient – and it gave me something concrete to work on. All I had to do was quicken up my starts and I could be among the leaders. I felt closer to my goals than ever before.

In Val d'Isère the previous December I had met a young Englishman doing a bit of freelance journalism on the World Cup circuit. His name was Mark Amis. He was very keen to see more of the races so I said to him: 'Why don't you come with me for a month in the car? You can stay in my room so it won't cost you much and you will get a chance really to see what this business is about from close up.'

Mark was enthusiastic about the idea but couldn't come with me immediately (that was the time I took my passportless American). Arrangements were made for me to pick him up later in the season and, after the Christmas break, we met in Alpbach. He was a tremendous help right from the word go. He knew absolutely nothing about skiing but was as keen as mustard to learn. I threw him in at the deep end. His hunger to learn helped him pick up the complexities of the sport very quickly and, after a time, he became my full-time assistant. We were a new concept in ski teams – in our case the racer was in charge of the trainer!

Despite his lack of experience, Mark's ability was quite incredible. The first day he was with me I sent him to a team captains' meeting. He went without knowing what to expect and represented me amongst all the heavies of skiing. It is to his credit that, although he was naturally wide-eyed, he did not allow the occasion to overawe him. He did the job that I asked of him and he did it well. It was not long before he had the respect of the other trainers on the hill.

For me he was invaluable. He would bring the skis down from the mountain at the end of the day, attend all the meetings, look after my race entries, oversee the servicing of my skis by the Swiss technician, and load and unload the car. He was tireless in his work and never complained once. He was much, much more than just my assistant – he was my friend. I could confide in him and unburden myself upon him whenever I felt the need. He always listened and he was always a support. It would be almost impossible to overestimate the value of his contribution to my crusade.

Unfortunately I couldn't have Mark on the team for the World Championships as I had already made arrangements with Peter. He was naturally disappointed but the disappointment quickly turned to smiles when the Canadian team asked for his help in their start crew. That was one huge feather in Mark's cap. The young English tenderfoot had done his job so well that, as soon as he was available, the Canadians, one of skiing's most prestigious teams, snapped him up. He thoroughly deserved that recognition and the experience he gained was tremendously beneficial to me when he rejoined me later.

The week before the World Championships, at the finish of the downhill at Kitzbühel, I had been approached by Brian James of the *Daily Mail*, who wanted an interview. As I had just finished a race, the adrenalin was flowing, and he caught me at my most acerbic. I let fly a little saying how ridiculous it was that the British team should be carrying such dead wood and things of that sort. It was a hard-hitting interview but it gave the truth as I saw it.

I heard nothing about the article until just before the start of the World Championship giant slalom. Ben Watson, the man who had replaced General Graeme as Federation General Secretary, skied over to me and complained that what I had said was not making it any easier for them to get support for the youngsters. I was tempted to ask him if he knew what the word support meant and whether he would consider supporting me. I was also tempted to congratulate him on his timing in accosting me just before a race. I did neither of these things: no amount of argument or caustic comment from me was going to change the views of so insensitive a person and I just couldn't be bothered.

When downhill time came I was really keyed up. Training had gone well and my skis were running: just the thought of the race made me quite high. Once I was going I wasn't going to let anything hold me back. I literally yelled encouragement to myself – something I had never done before and was not to do again – and I drove myself with fierce determination. For me the race was the most important of my life.

At the bottom I was seventeenth. Sepp Walcher was World Champion and Michel Veith runner-up. They were about three seconds ahead of me, but I had finished fifteen places better than the best official Briton, Alan Stewart. I was disappointed that I hadn't finished in the top fifteen as I had at St Moritz in 1974 but, all in all, both Peter and I were satisfied with the result. We had achieved most of what we set out to do.

Although the championships were a minor success for me, they were a disaster for the accredited British team. Afterwards, the Alpine Race Controller, Richard Berry, announced that he was resigning in protest at the style of management of Dieter Bartsch. In a letter to the Federation Richard said Dieter believed he should dictate to the controller how to run the team, despite the fact that Richard had a ton of experience. He also said that working with Dieter had made him see at first-hand 'why Bartelski and Fuchs rebelled'. He added that the Alpine Committee in London seemed ready to sacrifice anyone to ensure the continuation of Dieter as the team's technical director.

When I heard this news I was dumbfounded. After this and the results, surely they would start to realise what was happening and act. In fact no action took place for three months. It was incredible to me, particularly in a sport that measures its successes and failures in hundredths of seconds, that the Federation, with incontrovertible evidence staring them in the face, should take such an eternity to do anything. In the event their action was to refuse Dieter a renewal of contract. He was dropped.

When I heard this I was sure I would soon hear from the Federation asking for talks to reconcile our positions. No such request came. Instead my father and I went to London on our own initiative to talk to them. But this was not a father and son act. My father was representing me, not as a parent but as my counsel. At a meeting with the committee he spoke for me and put my position. It was just as well that he did because many of the committee's utterances would have sparked furious responses from me.

Their view was virtually unchanged. To them I was still a naughty boy who must change his ways before being allowed back. I must promise to accept the direction of the management without question and I must 'set a good example' to the youngsters.

It was ridiculous. In my own eyes I was far from being a naughty boy: my only crime was that I wanted to ski to the best of my ability. In my opinion I hadn't been the root of the problem – only the scapegoat for the failures of others.

As it turned out, though, the meeting was a big step in the right direction. It was agreed that I should rejoin the British team in a year's time. This would allow for a cooling-off period and would enable me to make the break with the Dutch slowly and tactfully. I still had to make my own way for the year but the ice was melting and the way was open for me to ski for my own country again.

That summer I continued my training alone. I did some technical training on the Val Senales glacier with the Dutch and there met up with a young Austrian who was racing under Luxembourg colours. His name was Marc Girardelli. It was ironic that we were training together on the same glacier, as Marc had also had trouble with his Federation and was skiing as a loner. The parallel was almost uncanny.

Most of my fitness training that summer involved long cycle rides from my parent's home base at Zell am See, but the real work began at Hintertux when I again joined the Austrians on the glacier. As with the previous year training went really well and I was optimistic that this was to be the year of the breakthrough.

I knew, however, that if I was going to make it I would have to have Mark Amis with me full-time – and this meant meeting double expenses. To do so I changed my ski company again. Alois Rohrmoser, the boss of Atomic, had told me that his company would give me skis, service and cash towards running expenses: an offer I couldn't refuse.

In many ways the 1978–79 season was an easier one for me. I no longer felt the need to prove myself to the British but, on the other hand, I found it increasingly difficult to justify my hand-to-mouth skiing. All the cash I had coming in was going into the sport. I travelled around in my ancient Lancia Fulvia coupé, laden to the gunwales with the paraphernalia necessary to keep myself going, and I often felt twinges of jealousy when I saw other racers arriving in BMWs with nothing aboard but personal effects – all their actual ski gear was looked after by team employees.

Increasingly during that year I asked myself if it was all worth it. Sometimes I even considered retirement. Mark and I made a very efficient little unit but we had to consider any purchase twice. We could never go to the newsagent and buy a good selection of papers: one newspaper a day was our ration. For me it was all very difficult to take but Mark, who revelled in the white circus life, kept me going. Whenever I got low and began talking about packing it in he would bring me back to earth. When I asked myself what the hell I was doing it for, it was Mark who would remind me that I was doing it because I loved it; that, like a drug, it was in my blood; as much a part of me as breathing.

On the skiing side I never got close to the breakthrough I had keenly anticipated in training. Twenty-fifth at Kitzbühel was the best I could do. I wasn't skiing badly and many of the problems were to do with skis that had been improperly tested and prepared. That I didn't pick this up sooner says nothing for my maturity in the sport – indeed it shows the extent to which I was still naive.

At the end of the season Mark and I flew to Vancouver for the last World Cup race. We had to meet the cost of Mark's fare ourselves but, when we got to British Columbia, the race was cancelled because of dangerous conditions. It was a damp-squib end to an unmemorable year. The only good thing to come out of it was a three-week holiday in Vancouver that we treated ourselves to once the race was cancelled. It was the first time we had been able to relax

LEFT Aged three – practising for *The Londoner* parties in Kitzbühel!

BELOW First photo on skis, at five years old. Kitzbühel 1959.

BOTTOM My first award, pinned on by Gitti Schatz. Kitzbühel 1962.

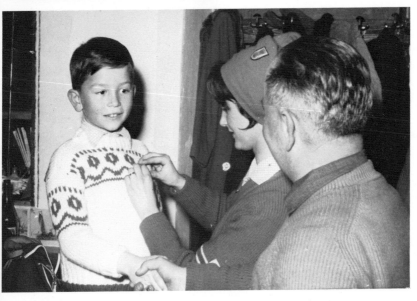

LEFT A classic position in the slalom; winning the British Junior Championships at Cairngorm in 1970.

BELOW The Three Musketeers with the famed Volkswagen. Left to right, Dieter Bartsch, Peter Fuchs, Willy Bailey and myself at Zell am See in 1973.

BOTTOM The end of our first season together – Peter Fuchs and me, again at Zell am See in 1973.

TOP LEFT Flying high: on the way to fifteenth place in the World Championships at St Moritz, 1974.
Colorsport

TOP RIGHT My first World Cup slalom, at Mürren in 1971. *Colorsport*

A good reason for my not specialising in slalom! Kitzbühel, 1973.
Colorsport

Megève, February 1975. (LEFT) Out of control . . . (BELOW) Unconscious . . .

Val Gardena, December 1981. Moment of truth – before (ABOVE) and after (RIGHT). At last the Union Jack flies above the podium.
Daniel Rose/J. Fausel

BELOW Smiles all round: in the background, the bump that cost me the race, the scoreboard that told me the good news, and (far left) David Vine looking for his story. I talk Koni Rupprechter (left) and Stuart Fitzsimmons through the race. *Daniel Rose*

Schladming, 1982, World Championship downhill. No 'second' chance . . .

A coat of varnish (skimming the safety net)

The costly correction . . .

Just made it, but seconds wasted. *Stuart Fitzsimmons*

LEFT Crans Montana, December 1981. Round one, racer v official! Serge Lange and I, face to face. *Walter Keller*

BELOW Round two, racer v mountain. Enjoying myself at Val d'Isère, in February 1983. *Colin Riddle/Club Mark Warner*

My last race, at Lake Louise, March 1983. (LEFT) Franz Klammer back on top, winning the World Cup – champagne presented by Ulli Forster. (BELOW) Ken Read and me, unemployed.

thoroughly for a long, long time. We behaved like tourists. We drank a few beers, went to the movies, played the odd game of tennis and went to parties. In those three weeks we both got used to waking up with hangovers but, for me, those bleary mornings with gongs clanging in my head and my tongue like a strip of emery cloth, were the very breath of spring. The holiday was like a luxurious bath. It washed away my lethargy and my tiredness, and when I got back to Europe I was hungry again. This time I could be hungry with John Bull on my side, too.

It was 1980, an Olympic year again, and this heightened my sense of nationalism. Being back in the British squad was strange. At first I missed my freedom and the little irritations that came with being back in the arms of the administrators irked perhaps more than they should. One of the problems was that I was still largely alone. Stuart Fitzsimmons had retired and there was no one on the team to whom I was close. I tried to get Mark Amis into the set-up by suggesting to Elspeth Crossley-Cooke, who had replaced George Stewart as Alpine chairman, that he would be a good person to have in British ski team management. Elspeth was sceptical: she was wary of having somebody around who was so unashamedly a Bartelski man! But at least we could discuss things constructively and I had a coach again. Koni Rupprechter, who after the demise of Dieter Bartsch had been made number one, didn't find it too difficult to bury all the old hatchets with me and we began to work well together.

Although we were getting on better on the social level, we were still unable to get it together on the hill. When I watched myself on video I could see nothing radically wrong. My position was quite tight and I was skiing good lines but I was unable to get the speed. On the flats at Wengen I was three seconds slower than the leaders. The problem, of course, was skis again, and when we went to North America to prepare for Lake Placid my ski bags were bulging with skis to test.

For this work we went to Hunter Mountain in New York State. There, in freezing temperatures and in thin racing suits, we tested skis non-stop. It is the most boring work that can be done in ski racing. Up, down, up, down . . . over and over again. By the time you have finished a day of it you are almost rigid with boredom and cold. But it pays dividends. In this particular testing session we discovered one pair of skis that were quick. It was a discovery that was to make all the difference to my Olympic campaign.

Before leaving for the Olympics I had been in two frames of mind: one hopeful, one uncertain. Because of the background work we had done I was hopeful; but there was uncertainty that, perhaps, this might be my last race. With the results I had been having I felt I couldn't justify continuing. Maybe I just wasn't going to make it; maybe the breaks just were not for me. I had already started looking at other possible avenues: working perhaps or maybe professional racing, I didn't know, but I had made up my mind that if my Lake Placid result wasn't any better than my European World Cup results I would have to find something else. It wasn't a pleasant prospect, I still hadn't achieved what I had set out to do, but the thought was there that perhaps I never would; that it was better to cut my losses and start afresh.

However, training for Lake Placid went smoothly and fast from the word go. The faster skis we had found in those long, boring, sessions of testing were still doing their stuff. I was now quicker on the flats – the part of the race where I had been much slower before – and my better end-race times were still holding up. It was so good to feel the skis run under me. To the layman it might sound ridiculous, but the difference between those skis and the ones I had been skiing on earlier was the difference between a bar-room honky-tonk piano and a concert grand. Instead of having to do all the work myself the skis took over from time to time. Every time I got on them I knew something was going to happen: they were a tonic for me and the key to my continuing skiing.

The contrast between Lake Placid and Sapporo was even more dramatic than that between Innsbruck and Sapporo. In Lake Placid, instead of having an Olympic village to stay in, we were put into a newly-built prison complex. It was to be one of those new, modern prisons with one prisoner to each cell – but in our case they started the ball rolling with a little good old-fashioned over-crowding, two to a cell!

Security was evident everywhere. Twice, while just jogging around the perimeter, I was stopped by policemen – and they were policemen a long way removed from the kindly English bobby helping old ladies over the road.

Of all the racers, the only one who liked the village set-up was Ingemar Stenmark. Ingemar hated intruders and he particularly hated the press. When he found himself in a compound that was difficult to get away from he was happy. If it was difficult for him to get out it must also be difficult for others to get in. For Stenmark it was a state of affairs close to pure bliss.

The Lake Placid downhill course was a bit like a bee who stings like a butterfly! The top part of the course, a series of sharp, icy bends that last for about thirty seconds, was quite testing and every skier had to be on his toes. But after those turns had been negotiated the course was flat and boring. If it hadn't been for the pop of flash bulbs I am sure I would have fallen asleep. It wasn't that the course was slow – there was a part where we were touching 90mph – but it was so smooth and undemanding that I, for one, was never really aware of the high speed. I felt the real course was over after the first thirty or forty seconds and that the rest was just a *schuss* to the line.

On race day there was some new snow on the course. So I tucked my head a little further down and skied with my skis just a little bit closer together than usual so that I could get them running on the glazed tracks of others, and not in the deeper snow which would have slowed them down with friction.

The actual *schuss* to the finish seemed to take an eternity but when I was finally through the gates I quickly looked back to see my time. I knew it was quite fast but there was no indication of what my position was. Because of this I wasn't able to build up any real excitement. It wasn't until I got down to the commentary box of David Vine that I realised I had come twelfth. David was pleased, as indeed was everyone else; I had finally broken Jeremy Palmer-Tomkinson's twelve-year record. In 1968 Jeremy had been twenty-fifth in Grenoble – a position that hadn't been beaten until now.

I found it difficult to match David's enthusiasm as I had not been able to pick any up in the finish area, but I was certainly pleased, especially as I was to go on skiing for another year. I could hardly give up now.

On the basis of my result Elspeth Crossley-Cooke decided it would be good for me to go down to New Zealand to get in some snow training in the southern hemisphere winter. I persuaded her to let me take Sigi Bernegger with me so that I would have a really experienced downhill coach, and the two of us set off in July for the slopes of the Southern Alps.

On the flight out we stopped over at Singapore for a couple of days to rest up, do some shopping and meet up with Ken Read. Ken was to join the Canadian team who were already in New Zealand but had decided to meet me first for the journey down.

Those two days in Singapore were good fun. I remember one night Sigi was attracted to a group of young girls hanging around outside the hotel. He was all set to go and chat one up until we told him they were all drag queens! At first he couldn't believe it – they were all too beautiful, he said. When the truth was out Sigi was a little taken aback. He was a policeman himself back in Austria and all he could say was: 'Thank goodness I don't have to put up with such problems on my own patch.' Sigi wasn't one to find much in common with the people who live on the periphery of society. He was a straight-up-and-down, no-holds-barred man who used a combination of discipline and knowledge to get what he wanted done. I knew that with him I had the chance to do some really constructive work.

At Mount Hutt, a marvellous bowl of snow overlooking the Canterbury plains with the glitter of the blue Pacific gleaming in the distance, we were to take part in a FIS downhill held over two legs. Although the Canadian team were there, along with the New Zealanders and the Australians, the race was something of a farmers' derby. I had a good run in the first leg of the race but Ken pipped me on the second. The overall result, however, was that I had beaten Ken by one-hundredth of a second.

Psychologically this was a most important win for me. In the preceding year Ken had won both the Lauberhorn and the Hahnenkamm and for me to beat him here was no small boost to my self-confidence. It's true it was a two-man race (even though Dave Irwin was with the Canadians he was not able to get close to us) and the locals were just pleased that we had chosen New Zealand to train so that their own boys could reap some benefit. Even so to beat Ken Read over the same course and over the same conditions was a real fillip for me. As my confidence started to flood back my brain kept saying things like 'if you can beat him here you can beat him anywhere', and 'if you can beat Ken Read you can beat anyone on the circuit'. It was wonderful. There I was, in one of the most beautiful countries in the world, once again charged with the belief that mounting the winner's podium was something not beyond me.-

After that the bite came back into my resolve. This year I was going to have a real go at cracking it.

When the training was over I suggested that we should have a short holiday in New Zealand but Ken vetoed this, saying we had been in the winter too long, it was time for us to get some summer sun. He wanted us to soak up a bit of the ultra-violet on Rarotonga and Tahiti. My problem was that I only had a ticket for Los Angeles and London; it wasn't valid for Pacific island stopovers. But after an hour on the telephone I changed my ticket for a round-the-Pacific route, ending up at Vancouver. From there I would fly on to London standby, the best way I could.

So, in August 1980, Ken and I set off from Auckland on an Air New Zealand DC10 for Rarotonga: and the holiday of our lives.

Suddenly we were in a land of no mountains, no snow and no hassles. In Rarotonga we found delicious white sand beaches, golden-skinned people who seemed to have either a smile or a song permanently on their lips, and the sense of peace that can only really come from being on a tiny island. We stayed four days in the Cook Islands – as long as the sale of one pair of skis would allow – before moving off to Tahiti, where a pair of skis lasted only a day!

It was a fantastic round trip and I had seen a great deal, but now all I could think of was getting down to work for the new season. As soon as I was back in London I started to get things moving, spending most of my time on the 'phone. Because of this I put off ringing Peter at Carrbridge. However, on about the third day, I got a strong, almost eerie, feeling and just had to ring him. We talked for an hour. He was happy, his wife and children were well, and he had just acquired a new Jaguar XJ12. He was jolly, bouncy and keen to hear all the stories of my trip, and his infectious breeziness found its way to me.

That was a Sunday night. I couldn't stay in London very long, as I had to go to Annecy to test boots for the Salomon factory, so I left on the Monday morning. The following morning, Tuesday, I had a telephone call from Mark Amis. He said: 'Peter . . .' My heart sank and I felt dizzy. I knew already what Mark was going to say. There had been a head-on car smash and Peter, in his sparkling XJ12, had been killed instantly.

It was the worst news I had ever had in my life. For about nine years Peter and I had been as close as brothers. More than that, we had been friends and colleagues in a sport not noted for very close friendships between racers. Ever since the Three Musketeer days we had shared each other's highs and lows. We had spurred each other on and supported each other whenever a bad patch came along. We were human, of course, and there were many times when we didn't quite see eye-to-eye, but those times were few and easily forgotten. All my memories of Peter are good ones: his talent, his love of fun, his loyalty as a friend and his willingness to put himself out are aspects of his personality that I shall always treasure. Without Peter there was something lacking, some element missing, from my skiing career. Put quite simply, I had lost my best friend.

My first impulse was to jump on a plane to go to Peter's wife and parents but I couldn't, at least for a short while, just drop my business with Salomon. I rang Peter's parents and my own – Peter's so that I could commiserate with them, and mine to give myself someone to talk to. Despite knowing many of the people at Salomon, Peter's death had made me feel quite alone.

As soon as my business was finished I took the first plane to London. I had booked to fly alone but I was pleased to find myself travelling with Peter Hankey from Salomon. His words of comfort were a godsend.

Once in London my first thought was to travel straight to Carrbridge but I had several long-standing engagements, some of which involved speaking to clubs, and I met all of these before travelling north. Naturally the temptation was there to cancel them, but I knew Peter would have disapproved of that and I knew he would have wanted me to carry on and get on with achieving the goals I had set myself. Peter was on my mind throughout those few days and I finally got up to Carrbridge on the morning of Thursday, the day of the funeral.

When I got back to the snow at Hintertux after the funeral nothing was quite the same. Memories of Peter were everywhere and racing friends, young and old, kept coming up to me to say how sorry they were. Everyone was very kind but all I wanted to do was get on with the job. Years before Peter and I had started along a road and now I wanted to finish the journey – for his sake as much as mine. To do this I had to train harder than ever before, reach hitherto undiscovered levels of determination, and show the world that the dreams we had had as young boys starting out could be realised.

The season itself started quite well for me. In the December 1980 downhill at Val d'Isère I was eighteenth and, at Val Gardena a week later, I managed sixteenth, just two-hundredths of a second off a World Cup point. I was still knocking on the door but I never seemed able to do any more than that. The other races on the European downhill circuit saw me hovering round the low twenties and I couldn't see any improvement in sight when I left for Aspen in March 1981 for the American races.

It was the first time I had been to Aspen, and I was quite excited. Just before departure, too, I had been approached by Rothmans, who wanted to know if I would do some rally driving for them. Motor sport had always been my second love and to be asked to rally for Rothmans made me very chuffed indeed.

I had, of course, heard a great deal about Aspen. Only a short time before I had seen it written up in the *News of the World* under the banner 'Aspen, Sex and Drugs and Rock and Roll' and I wanted to see this so-called Sodom-and-Gomorrah town for myself. It was the last race of the season (the traditional time for parties and high jinks) and the prospect of enjoying this in a town of ninety bars and countless night clubs was intoxicating.

In the race I was twenty-fourth – still knocking on heaven's gate and getting no reply.

I may have let myself down in the race, but the coloured-light and tinsel town of Aspen didn't let any of us down when it came to whooping-up time. In a whirl of parties, with almost the fury of the legendary dervish, I threw the cares and troubles of 1980–81 out of the window. By the time I left that hedonists' town my slate had been wiped clean ready for the season to come.

Summer training was again on the other side of the world. The Federation had agreed to send a party of boys to Australia and New Zealand and I worked hard to get them flight arrangements that would let them see something of that delightful corner of the planet.

Despite my efforts to show them Hawaii en route, the other boys in the team seemed to take the whole thing in a very matter-of-fact manner. I had been to these places before yet I felt I was more excited about being on the other side of the world than they were. Their attitude didn't seem a good omen for the races to come.

In the event this was true for me, but not for the others. Martin Bell and Freddie Burton raced really well in New Zealand and it was me who was out of it. I had been trying an experiment on a pair of boots which, although I sorted it out on the morning of the race, took me in completely the wrong direction for most of the training. I did nothing in the race and I had lost a lot of my edge.

Things were a bit different in Australia. Up in the Snowy Mountains I met many old friends, some of whom I hadn't seen for nine years. Their company became more important to me than the rigours of training and I was constantly breaking the curfew rules as I stayed out with them, rapping about old times. I was relaxed, almost lethargic by my own standards, and that visit to the Antipodes is remembered more for the socials than for the skiing.

When I returned to England, Rothmans put me under the wing of Brian Culcheth to be coached in rally driving. For me this was an eye-opener. It was a thoroughly professional group, well-organised and brilliantly coached by Brian. We travelled all over Britain driving on circuits and in forests and I was really getting on in this new sport. I liked the sense of purpose and the professionalism. I liked having a budget that allowed me to choose the steak instead of the hamburger and I liked the thrill of learning a totally new discipline. Every now and again I would leave to do my required ski training, but I always looked forward to returning to Brian and the cars. Under his expert tuition my concentration and co-ordination improved. I saw a sports psychologist who gave me insights into the effect of the mind on the body in high-speed sports, and I was checked out for physical fitness and stamina.

The rally course came to an end in October with a test around the forest stages of Wales. I was more than a little sorry when I waved them goodbye to take up full-time skiing again in preparation for the first World Cup downhill at Val d'Isère. I only hoped that there would be a little of the professionalism I had just left behind waiting for me within the ski team management.

Training this time was mainly at Kaunertal, near Landeck in Austria, and I approached it in quite a relaxed manner. Freddie Burton was beating me consistently in training but I wasn't worried and continued working on one thing at a time. It was a period of consolidation.

After Kaunertal there was a short session at Obertauern where we encountered very hard, icy conditions. We were training with the Americans and I noticed that the faster the course got the faster my form improved. I didn't know it at the time but it was this combination of fast track training and improving form that was to take me on to Val Gardena.

If there has been a pattern in my skiing career it is that whenever I feel confident a period of depression arrives. It was after the much more encouraging Obertauern training that my race form hit rock-bottom, with the sixty-first in Val d'Isère. Perhaps if I hadn't hit the cataclysmic low that this result produced I would not have been able to rise the very next week, at Val Gardena, to my second placing: the result that I had been working for since Gitti Schatz first initiated me into ski racing.

— 6 —
ACCIDENTS AND INJURIES

Everybody who takes up ski racing – whether it be slalom, giant slalom or downhill – expects to crash. It is part of the sport. Ski racing is fast, and racers have to push themselves to the limits of their physical and mental endurance in their quest for results. At such speeds, and with such a tiny margin for error (in some cases no margin at all), mistakes are made: and in ski racing mistakes mean crashes. It is as simple as that.

I have heard some people say that if it wasn't for crashes public interest in ski racing would be zero. This may well be so. It may be that all sports which combine skill with high speed, such as motor racing, speedway, powerboat racing and the like, acquire their following due to the public's blood-lust. But really it is irrelevant to ask if the sport would appeal to the public without the thrill of crashes – the only question that is important is: 'If there were no crashes, would there be any racers?'

For a ski racer, the only measure of blowing it, of pushing too hard and going over the top, is to crash out. Crashing is a way of learning: a way of discovering personal limits. A racer who has never crashed is not even within sight of his limits or his potential, while a racer who crashes continually is trying to do more than his physical limitations will allow.

In my own early days of skiing I hardly knew what a crash was. Oh, I had fallen down often enough and I had experienced the pain that can come from a badly fitted ski-boot, but I had never experienced the agony that can follow a spinning, thumping crash at 50mph-plus. That experience didn't come until downhill training at Val d'Isère in 1971.

On that occasion I had borrowed Royston Varley's skis for the day and was just passing the 'S' turns by the meadows, halfway down the course, when my right ski hit a bump hard. The force was such that the binding opened and the ski clattered ahead of me. All would have been fine if the riderless ski had bounced out of the way. Instead it did the opposite and ricocheted into my track, slicing into my left shin, It was the first time I had drawn blood; as a ski racer I had finally lost my cherry!

Despite the injury I gathered myself together, collected my skis, and skied gingerly down to the bottom. I never fancied the prospect of a bumpy journey down in a blood-wagon and, indeed, have never had one. My crashes have either been minor enough to allow me to get away under my own steam or so serious that I have had to be lifted off the mountain in a helicopter – unfortunately so far out of it that I was unable to enjoy the view.

The helicopter rescue came after a fall at Megève in February 1975. It was a World Cup downhill and I was racing with my wrist still heavily bandaged from a fall I had had at Morzine the previous month. There I had completely mistimed a jump, and came down heavily in a heap. When I sat up I knew something was wrong even though I could feel no pain and, sure enough, as soon as I was examined, a broken wrist was revealed: my first ever broken bone. The wrist was plastered and I had returned to the team's quarters only to have Dieter inquire if I was racing the next day. It would have been a good joke if he hadn't been serious. That incident, though, was nothing compared with Megève: the *pièce de résistance* fall of my career.

Megève had long been a bogey course, and had killed the French racer, Michel Bozon, in 1970. After his death the course had been modified somewhat and, if anything, made too simple for a World Cup downhill. Indeed I and several other racers complained that, apart from a jump over a road, the course was just a simple run down from top to bottom. As usual these criticisms fell on deaf ears and the race was on.

I was in the second group and I drew sixteen, the starter immediately after the first group of skiers. I took this to be a good omen, but in fact it was the opposite. On the next two occasions on which I drew sixteen I also fell, and the time came when I dreaded the prospect of drawing it – fortunately I never got it again.

For the Megève race, low cloud and light snow began to close in just as I was about to go. The organisers wanted to postpone the start for the second group, but I knew that so much new snow would by then be on the course that speeds would be slowed down and there would be no chance of getting close to the first group. So I persuaded the starter to let me go anyway.

Before I went Dieter had warned me on the radio to take the jump over the road very carefully. Several skiers, including Bernard Russi, had crashed there, and I was to treat it with caution. In practice I had measured my approach to the jump quite well but the French organisers, for reasons known only to themselves, changed the nature of the bump every day. This meant that no matter how much it was practised it was impossible to know exactly how the jump would ski.

In my case I pre-jumped the road, landed a little short with the ends of my skis clipping the road surface, and plummeted head first into the shallow slope below. That was the last thing I remembered.

Some hours later I woke up in hospital, and was visited by Peter Fuchs and his girlfriend. The first thing I wanted to know was how I had done. I had no idea if I had finished the race – I may even have won it for all I knew – and I had no idea of the extent of my injuries.

As soon as Peter's girlfriend came into the room she put her hand to her face in an attempt to block out mine. Instinctively I reached up and touched my own and realised I was disfigured. Only then did it dawn on me that I had had a serious crash. I asked Peter to tell me all about it.

Apparently after my skis had hit the road I began to do head-over-heels cartwheels with my limbs twisting and contorting every time I hit the surface of the course. For me it was all over in a flash, as I must have been unconscious from the first contact with the ground; but for the public on the course, as well as millions of television viewers all over Europe, the fall presented a horrifying spectacle.

When my body came to a halt in a crumpled heap, officials pulled me clear to the side of the course and there I remained for a full threequarters of an hour. In that time the crowd were offering odds on whether I was alive or dead. Even in our own house in Zell am See my parents put my chances at fifty-fifty. They must have been worried sick, first watching the crash and then having to wait so long to find out that I was all right: but it took me a long time to understand the extent of their suffering on that day.

For me the day was no problem; one of my easiest in skiing. First I was racing, and then I was in bed. I didn't even have to take my racing suit off!

Several people have asked me since if I considered giving up afterwards, and I can honestly say that I did not. I didn't remember the crash and, apart from feeling sore, I had no other ill effects. There had been no time for me to be frightened – I had been rendered unconscious too early for that – and I had not lost my nerve, so there was no question of giving up. Even when I saw a playback of the fall on television I found it hard to realise that the cascading puppet on the screen was me: it was more as though I was watching a drama production.

In the event, my injuries were nowhere near as serious as the film indicated. I had a twisted and bruised knee which I hardly noticed, my face was swollen and bruised (so much so that it got in the way when I spoke), and I had severe concussion. I was very lucky.

One of the more peculiar aspects of the crash was that, although I was unconscious until about six o'clock, I spent the time before that translating for Dieter and the medical staff. Dieter spoke no French and they no English, so I, with my mind not registering on the conscious level at all, apparently served as interpreter!

After a week I was finally allowed out into the world for the journey home, and it was only then that I realised how much effect the crash had had. Everybody recognised me, everyone stared, or wanted to know how I was. At last British skiing was on the map: the rub being that it was through a spectacular crash and not a victory! I should have picked this up when I was visited by the Italian racer, Erwin Stricker, in hospital. Erwin's view was simple: I had made it. He said to me: 'A good crash is better than coming second any day. People won't forget this for many, many years.' He was right. Even as late as the 1982–83 season, race commentators were still referring to it and World Cup television viewers in Switzerland and Austria still took special note of my efforts in case they should see a repeat performance!

Although I achieved some fame with my Megève fiasco it was nothing to that acquired by the Swiss racer, Roland Collombin, at

Val d'Isère. In 1974, Roland had mistimed a pre-jump on the course, lost his balance in the air and come down on the ends of his skis. He fell and was lucky not to do himself an injury. But the following year (the year Michel Dujon killed himself in Tignes) the Val d'Isère course was a real nightmare. Of the ninety skiers who started training for the race only about sixty actually started – the rest having been put out by accident or nerves. One of those put out by an accident was Roland. At exactly the same bump that had caught him out the previous year, he mistimed and then froze in the air. I was watching from the sidelines because I had hurt my knee at Lienz the week before and, in an earlier training session on the same day, had come to grief at the same bump. Unfortunately for him, Roland's fall relegated mine into the 'slip and slide' category.

After losing his confidence and freezing, Roland dropped onto the hard-packed snow of the course with his skis perpendicular to the running surface. The force of the impact catapulted him into the air and he hit the course again in a series of sickening thumps. For me it was like watching in slow motion. I had known Roland was in trouble from the moment he began the jump. His progress, from that moment on, seemed to be at snail's-pace to me; I could almost feel every twist, every impact. I knew he was hurt badly. In fact he spent several months in hospital. He didn't break his back but it was a close thing, and he was lucky to avoid having to spend the rest of his life in a wheelchair.

But, as Erwin Stricker said, a fall is good for fame. From that moment on the bump that had caught Collombin out on two successive years became known as the *Bosse à Collombin*. He achieved renown but at what cost: Roland never raced again.

Ski racers have to be like motor racing drivers after a bad crash. If you dwell on the tragedy too much your racing edge is lost and you cease to be competitive. It is necessary to put the effect of somebody else's fall behind you as soon as possible and, with your own falls, you must get back on skis as soon as you can. Like horse riders, the quicker you are back in the saddle the less chance there is that you will lose your nerve.

After a while, of course, racing tumbles become part of life and you develop a certain skill in dealing with them. For most spectators, downhill crashes seem to happen very fast – not surprising perhaps when the racer may be going 60mph – but for the skier there is actually time to think. As soon as you become aware that you are going, the first thing to do is look forward, to make sure there are no trees or rocks immediately ahead. Sometimes, but by no means always, it is possible to change the direction of the fall to avoid such disaster zones. If, however, and this has happened to me a couple of times, all you can see is the sky, the trick is to relax as much as possible. If you can do this successfully the chance of serious injury on impact is greatly reduced. The idea is to try to fall as if you were drunk. Intoxicated people rarely hurt themselves when they fall because the alcohol has relaxed the muscles so much that the body absorbs the force of the fall evenly. Of course ski racers fall much harder than the average drunk, but the same basic principle applies: the more you can relax, the safer you will be.

No matter how relaxed the fall, however, it is no good unless the skis release properly from the bindings. Flailing skis that remain attached to the boots are the commonest cause of lasting injury for a racer. Not only does the cartwheeling body come into sharp contact with these cumbersome things on the end of the legs, but there is also a chance that the torque the skis impose on the knees will pull the joints apart.

Bindings always pose a dilemma to downhillers. If they are loose, the skis will release cleanly in a fall but they are also more likely to come off when you do not want them to. If, on the other hand, they are tightened so that nothing short of a nuclear blast will release the skis, there is little chance of losing them in a race but there is a greatly increased chance of doing yourself damage in a fall. Obviously there is a happy medium, but it is such a fine line that it is not always possible to find it.

So, by relaxing and having properly adjusted bindings a ski racer can lessen the risk of injury. The only other thing that can be done is for the organisers to make sure that the course itself is as safe as possible.

First and foremost, the race organisers must make sure that the track is in good condition from the very first day of training. A few seasons ago the first group of downhillers tended to be virtually decimated by accidents, many of these being caused by slapdash course preparation. A modern ski race is 'on' from the first training session, and it is up to the officials to make sure that the running surface is smooth, fast and safe.

Course maintenance on the flat sections is easy. Caterpillar-tracked machines literally pummel the snow until it is smooth and wrinkle-free. The steeper sections are somewhat more difficult. There, small armies of men are needed to trample the course into shape, slowly and painstakingly. First ski boots are used to pack the snow, and then skiers climb up the hill sideways-on in tiny steps to smooth it out. Any holes that are left after this process are filled in with shovels, while any bumps that are too sharp and vicious are rounded off in the same way. It is a time-consuming operation but it must be done every night after training and checked again every morning. Only in this way can racers be spared accidents not of their own making.

Another way that the organisers can make a racer's life easier is with sensible and efficient use of crash barriers. There was a time when these were invariably bales of straw, which sometimes caused more injuries than they saved. It is in the very nature of skiing that it is a winter sport. In winter it snows and, if straw bales have been built up at critical positions on a race course, they get snowed on too. If the following day is warm, the snow melts into the straw and freezes again when the temperature drops at night. The straw bales thus take on the consistency of concrete and become useless for softening the impact of a fall.

A much better device is a safety net, and these are being used more and more on modern courses. The nets absorb the speed of a crash well and are easily the best things to hit if you must hit something. Not, of course, that it is a comfortable experience hitting a net at 80mph or so, but at least you know that you stand a good chance of getting up and walking away.

Naturally the organisers cannot completely line a race track with crash nets, and most courses still have some sections that are protected by straw. If it is fresh then there is no problem.

For example, at the Lauberhorn race at Wengen in 1981, Peter Müller crashed literally within yards of the finish. He mistimed the final jump so badly that he was thrown into a sitting position on the back of his skis. His speed and momentum prevented him from retrieving the situation and he crashed into the straw bales. He hit them like a racing car, and television audiences all over the world thought he must have done himself some terrible injury. In fact, because the straw was fresh and soft, all he suffered was a broken collar-bone.

By contrast, the Italian racer, Sigi Kerschbaumer, had a rather unexciting fall after losing an edge at St Anton in the same year, but crashed into bales that had frozen. Instead of saving him they halted his momentum so abruptly that he fractured his back and was lucky not to have suffered worse.

The sites of both of these crashes are now protected with more effective safety fences, but as I have said there is still straw to be found somewhere on most downhills, and racers need to think twice before allowing themselves to plough into it.

The last word on safety matters for any race comes from the jury. This group of five people decide when the course becomes unsafe, and when to stop or restart the training or racing. It is a pretty reliable system and, by and large, responsible decisions are taken. But not always.

At Sarajevo in Yugoslavia in 1983 the track was running so fast that racers were coming off bumps at such speed that they were being carried into hollow sections before landing. The result was that the body sustained a crushing, jolting impact as soon as the skis hit the ground. As the landing was effectively also a brake, the legs were thrown forwards and downwards into the boots, squashing the toes and putting unreasonable stress on the knees.

This was obviously an unsatisfactory state of affairs. Many racers were complaining of sore feet and legs, but the jury refused to stop the training. They also refused to round off the bumps that were causing the trouble. Their refusal resulted in ten practice injuries – including a major prang suffered by Peter Müller, who had to be flown home to a hospital in Switzerland – and many, many falls. The organisers let their sense of urgency for completing a pre-Olympic race overcome their concern for the safety of the participants. It was an example of the sort of callousness the sport can well do without.

Another cause of injury to racers has come from the development of modern boots. In the old days, when racers wore flexible boots, the ankle was able to work with the knee in the shock absorbing process. Now that boots are high and rigid, with the ankles held virtually immobile within, all the pressure and strain is being taken by the knees.

It is hard for somebody who hasn't been involved in ski racing really to understand just how wearing this constant stress is. Day in and day out the knees take the weight of the whole body as it rattles over bumps and rutty terrain. The cartilages tend to get compressed within the kneecap and the tendons and ligaments stretch so that they cannot do their job as effectively as they should. Because of this constant pounding, many racers suffer the agony of frequent knee operations during their racing careers. Fortunately I am not one of them – my knees have stood up well and, except for the bone spur operation, I have been spared knee trouble. But some friends of mine have not been so lucky. Steve Podborski has had three major knee operations and American Andy Mill, who was sixth in the Olympics in 1976, holds the record with thirteen operations to his legs. After the last one Andy was still keen to come back but his doctor (orthopaedic surgeon Dick Steadman, who has made a special study of ski injuries and who performed a minor miracle on Phil Mahre's ankle), told him that if he did there could be no guarantee that he would walk if he had another fall.

Medical science has certainly advanced a long way since I first took up racing, but it still helps if you're a little mad! It was no accident, for instance, that the Canadians acquired the title 'Crazy Canucks' – and of them Dave Irwin was by far the craziest.

Dave had won the 1975 World Cup downhill at Schladming and was skiing like a man possessed, but, one month later at Wengen, still with the demon inside him, he was wiped out in a major way.

In the first race he was seconds ahead of anyone else and was really smoking down the course. But he oversmoked it. In the last turn he was so fast his skis actually rode up onto a safety fence in the manner of a circus 'wall of death' rider. The mistake cost him about ten places, but he finished. In the second race he wasn't so lucky. Still going as though the hound of the Baskervilles was after him, he crashed on the Hundschopf. It was one of those crashes that even racers talk about. The Hundschopf is a treacherous jump with an approach only twelve feet wide, right next to a crowding rocky cliff. It is a mean little jump at the best of times but, for this race, Dave made it into a monster. He took a very risky direct line over the jump and lost control. In the ensuing crash he fell headlong down the mountain, finishing up in a heap almost on the railway tracks that lead to Kleine Scheidegg.

He suffered severe bruising and equally severe concussion – the worst injury a skier can have because, although it is serious, the racer tends to come back too soon and do himself further damage. Dave did just that, and went on to ski in the Olympics at Innsbruck only a fortnight later. He did quite well there but had another nasty fall in practice. I remember watching him stand up afterwards as if he didn't know what year it was. It was a lesson for me. I had had my own share of concussion, but seeing Dave force himself so hard and risk his body for the lack of a couple of weeks rest made me realise that racing injuries were things to take seriously.

There are, however, lighter moments in ski accidents – at least if you have a sickish sense of humour. At Val Gardena in 1977 I was watching the training runs on the video with members of the Canadian team. It was one of those years when the course was catching everyone out and there was a crash every second or third run. It was hilarious, we were rolling about on the floor as those guys tumbled down the mountain. Inside we knew it could have been any of us but it didn't stop us laughing at the cascading misfortune on the screen. In one incident an American came down, crashed, and fractured his spine. The blood wagon turned up to take him to hospital but, as they were taking him down on the sled, the next racer caught them up, lost control himself, and crashed into one of the rescue team, damaging *his* spine. So racer and rescuer ended up in adjoining beds, keeping each other company for a couple of weeks!

It was that young racer's first year in World Cup, and it was also his last. He was one of the phalanx of young boys who turn up only to disappear almost immediately. Sometimes it is a sort of fear – a realisation that they are risking themselves for nothing – and sometimes it is pressure from family or girlfriend, but many racers, some quite talented, have lost their appetite or their body after a season and called it a day.

The following year, 1978, at Val Gardena I took the Camel Bumps quite well but, as I landed hard on the third one almost immediately after taking off from the second, I felt an excruciating pain in my right foot. It was so bad that I had to pull to the side and stop. Examination revealed that I had landed on a stone. The impact had scarred my ski right through to the metal, and the force of my own weight within the boot had completely crushed the sole housing – of boots that were made for races and designed to take severe strain! My heel was so badly bruised from the incident that I could take no further part in the race, so I watched the others from a position just below the Camel Bumps.

Pretty soon Dave Irwin came down. As usual he was going hell for leather, but he took off from the second bump slightly off line. If he had landed where his skis were taking him he would have landed on a grass patch (the snow was very thin that year and the first group racers had worn away what little there was). To avoid the grass he tried to change direction in the air which was a disaster. On landing, all his weight was on his right foot. It was too much, and his leg simply crumpled underneath him, throwing his body onto the third bump.

It was almost as if he had been fired from a cannon. The terrible force of his body hitting the ground and the sheer speed at which he was travelling combined to shoot him about twenty feet into the air. Skis and bits of body were everywhere, and I can still hear the sickening thud as he hit the ground for the second time. But even more clearly than the thud I can hear the silences: the silence as his body seemed to hover grotesquely in the air before crashing, and the silence of the crowd after it was all over. It was one of those events that are so dramatic that the shock virtually paralyses everybody who witnesses it. Even Dave's trainers were not able to react quickly. It was probably only seconds, but it seemed like minutes before the scene started to come alive and people rushed over to see to his injuries. He was black and blue from head to foot and was again concussed.

The fact that Dave's trainers didn't react quickly infuriated me. Okay, Dave had blown his part of the operation, but the trainers were there to look after him, success or failure. A really brave racer was lying on that hill after giving every ounce of his energy for his country, and I was really shocked to see so little sense of urgency.

Ultimately, of course, crashes are the racer's alone. Everyone who races does so knowing that crashes are inevitable, but the urge, not to say the need, to race is so strong that they are accepted as part of the job.

In my own case, one of the biggest challenges in skiing was the Hahnenkamm at Kitzbühel. It was a course I loved to ski yet it was also one that had trapped me in each of its many snares. In my time I have fallen everywhere it is possible to fall at Kitzbühel – and some places where it isn't possible – but that course always called me back. Like Dave Irwin, Uli Spiess, Peter Müller, Andy Mill and all the other happy lunatics who called this their sport, I was content doing what I wanted. If I crashed, I crashed. *C'est la vie*. The first question I always asked afterwards was 'How soon can I go back?'

— 7 —
HIGH-TECH IN DOWNHILL

As well as in the obvious matter of speed, almost everything in ski racing is comparable to motor racing. The skis themselves are like the engine, responding to tuning in exactly the same way; the boots, and the fine tolerances between the angles, serve as the suspension, while the knees are the shock absorbers. When a skier's body is in the tuck position, aerodynamically it is doing precisely the same job as the shape of a Grand Prix car. The various preparations that can be put on the running surface of skis do the same job as different compounds of racing tyres. In motor racing some tyres suit dry conditions and some suit wet, so in skiing some preparations are best in dry, light snow and others work only when the snow is warm and melting.

What this means is that skiing is a highly technical sport. If the same skier uses two different pairs of skis on the same line and in the same snow conditions, the difference in times at the end of the run can vary by several seconds because of differences in the way the skis are made and the types of wax used. Such differences are so small as to be indiscernible, but, when you consider that just half a second can make the difference between first and fifteenth, it is not surprising that ski companies spend small fortunes on getting their skis and their waxing right.

The problem, of course, in growing up as a ski racer in the British team was that access to knowledge of the complicated technical details that make skis run well was denied to us. We were out of the main stream and we were naive. The attitude was that if you had a pair of skis and a hill you should be able to ski as fast as anyone else; if you didn't, it was because the others were better than you. It was somehow un-British and unsportsmanlike to blame the equipment, and for years we made no headway at all because we put all our defeats down to lack of talent and not lack of technical knowledge.

It was a bit like saying that if Divina Galica had put her foot down harder when she was driving Formula One for Hesketh, she could have won the championship. Divina may have lacked that sharp edge of talent to get her to the top even if she was driving a McLaren but, whether she had the talent or not, she could never have made it in the Hesketh: the car was simply uncompetitive. So it was with the skis that the British skiers were using – even worse in fact. For us it was like attempting to win a Grand Prix in a go-kart.

Of course, this is not to say that the British skiers would automatically have become winners if they had suddenly found themselves skiing on Franz Klammer's skis – but the chances are that they would have produced better times and they would have had the opportunity to develop their talents properly.

Even now the necessity of getting state-of-the-art technology for British ski racers isn't thoroughly understood by many of the administrators of the sport. It cannot be over-stressed that to do well in the sport you have to have the equipment and you have to have the mechanics.

In my own case, although I got skis and some technical support in my early years, it wasn't until Atomic made Ernst Habesatter available to me as a full-time technician in Val Gardena that I was able to come up with a first grade result.

Downhill skis are considerably different from the skis used for recreational skiing. They are longer, usually between 220 and 225 centimetres, and they are heavier to give them better tracking ability. Because the turns made in downhill are usually longer than in regular skiing, the side-cut of the ski, the narrowing at the waist, is much less pronounced.

All the downhill racing ski manufacturers adopt these basic criteria, but each varies them slightly to meet the company's own design philosophy. Fractionally more or less side-cut, an ounce or two more or less in weight, and different combinations in stiffness and flex make the differences in the models.

On paper, these seem nothing. Just as on paper motor racing cars can seem to have power and power-to-weight figures that are hard to separate. It is on the course and on the circuit that the little differences transform themselves into seconds. As in motor racing, every year a ski manufacturer finds a new secret, a new ingredient that may give his products the edge. It is a never-ending process of improvement and refinement, but it is expensive: so expensive, in fact, that the top skis and the top mechanics can only go to the top racers.

To the casual spectator it may seem that all skiers on Blizzard, for instance, have an equal chance. Not so. Although the skis have the same cosmetics, there are few similarities between a Blizzard ski of a top fifteen racer and a Blizzard ski skied by someone starting at sixty-one. The really 'hot' skis are put aside at the factory by those who know what they are looking for, and they go only to the top guys, the skiers who are proven fast and who are virtually carrying the flag for the company.

The combination of elements that make a ski hot are as complicated as the most elaborate Escoffier recipe, but there are people in the industry with eyes and hands so skilled that they can spot these skis when they come off the press. Only one in a hundred pairs of skis might meet the delicate balance required for excellence – but they are to be found, and they are better. It is a matter of fact.

But the real difference between winners and losers is in the ski base. To get this right the manufacturers test their products exhaustively over and over again. Sometimes racers on a company's books will be flown by helicopter straight from one race to test skis for the next. These test tracks are usually straight running courses of about thirty seconds duration. A tester will take a variety of skis and run them, top to bottom, over and over again. While this is happening technicians will be measuring acceleration times and speed at various points on the track. They will also be taking snow and air temperatures and noting the size and texture of the snow crystals.

Some of the skis will have been ground and prepared better than others and these will be the ones that are fast, but it may be that they only prove so in the conditions encountered on that day of testing. I remember that my Atomic skis were running very well in the year of Val Gardena but, when we took them to America for the races there, only one pair out of more than fifty would run. It was exasperating. Ski manufacture is such an exact science that some factories have special departments which do nothing else but study why some run fast and others do not.

Of course it is possible to have a good pair of skis botched by bad base preparation. An obvious fault is to put on the wrong wax for the type of snow, but many more fundamental mistakes can be made. The skis must be ground flat and the edges must be sharp but, surprising to some people, the running surfaces must not be too smooth. A good technician will run a wire brush over the base during preparation to roughen it slightly. This has the effect of breaking down the dragging vacuum that can form underneath a smooth ski, and allows the ski to run with minimal resistance.

Thus it is very important to have a good working relationship with your ski technician. Even more than that, it is important for the technician to feel he is an integral and important part of the team. In the 1982–83 season the Swiss were so successful because their head coach, Karl Fresner, brought all his racers and technicians together and got them working as one team. The fact that the racers skied on different brands of skis was unimportant to Fresner, he just wanted his team to be winners, and the technicians joined in with this spirit. All the training and testing was done together. The times and the testing information were available to everyone, and the close team bonds thus developed meant all the racers and all the technicians helped each other to common goals. Naturally there was still company rivalry when it came to race day, but because of the spirit and co-operation within the team the Swiss had more successful days than anyone else – and particularly more than their closest rivals, the Austrians.

In the Austrian camp there was no such co-operative outlook. Their ski rooms were secretive places, with company technicians hiding themselves in corners doing their thing on their own without consultation. The rivalry between the companies and between the racers was so strong that effective communication was impossible: the camp was more like a group of warring factions than a team. It was only the genius of Franz Klammer, skiing with all the panache of his 1976 triumph, that saved the day for the Austrians. Klammer won the overall title by two-hundredths of a second in the last race at Lake Louise. He started last of the first fifteen and 'stole' the race from Conradin Cathomen of Switzerland – but the Swiss were still the more consistent throughout the season.

My own experiences with the technical aspects of skis have been marked by feeling in the dark and lost opportunities. I started my skiing on Kneissl, but with neither factory back-up nor support. In those days I had to do all my own tuning and race preparation. It was like a reasonably competent home mechanic trying to tune a grand prix car. I wasn't up to date with the technology, and I lacked the expertise and 'feel' that goes into effective ski preparation. Because of the intense rivalry in the sport no one was going to tell me or show me what should be done, and I had to put my skis on the race courses on a trial-and-error basis.

When I changed to Blizzard in the 1974-75 season I was promised better equipment and more in the way of factory technical back-up. It never came. They had promised me race-tested skis and access to the factory's know-how, but in fact all I got was the skis.

Two months after the St Moritz World Championships in 1974 Fischer, another Austrian ski manufacturer, approached me, rather casually, to see if I would be interested in skiing on their skis. At the time they were producing quite good slalom and giant slalom skis but they did not have a reputation for making really fast downhill skis. Consequently I opted for Blizzard which was a big mistake. The following year Fischer swept the board with Klammer. It is interesting to note, though, that of all the Fischer skis Klammer had in that year of success, one pair was outstandingly fast. On this pair he won his races, and they were guarded as though they were a national treasure. Certainly they attracted more security than poor old Shergar apparently did, and that fine horse was worth, at a conservative estimate, several millions of pounds!

From that success Fischer went on to dominate ski racing for several years and they were a company that operated in a professional and practical way. Blizzard, on the other hand, never developed this professionalism and, compared with Fischer, their skis were usually counted among the also-rans.

Despite the fact that some skis run faster than others, it is the boots that most racers regard as their most prized and personal piece of equipment. Most recreational skiers put on ski boots for two weeks a year and even those who claim to have comfortable ones are glad to take them off at the end of the day and to give their feet a rest at the end of the holiday. Racers get no such relief. During the course of a season of racing, training and testing, a race skier will spend about nine months in his boots. It is essential that they must be comfortable but, even more important, they must offer the support necessary to cope with the forces and stresses that come from skiing to the limit.

The boots must have the right amount of forward lean for the skier, and they must be canted so that he can get his skis perfectly flat on the snow. The boots should also absorb most of the shocks of a race and, for this to happen, must have just the right degree of stiffness and not too much forward lean. If the canting isn't correct it can mean, as Steve Podborski found out to his sorrow, that the skier catches his edges a lot; and at the speeds achieved in downhill a caught edge usually spells instant disaster.

If there is anything that has nearly put me off skiing altogether, it is boots. I started in lace-up leather boots a full inch too long for me that had been passed down from my brother. The blisters and the soreness suffered because of them is still a painful memory. To get any degree of control those boots had to be done up so tight that my feet were screaming to get out. They were so uncomfortable that I saved up my pocket-money until I could afford a pair of leather clip boots. Compared with the old ones the new clip-ups were heaven, but compared with the modern boots of today they were a Model T Ford to a Lagonda.

In those days boots offered very little support. They had low backs and, because they were leather, they flexed sideways as well as forwards.

In 1968, when Jean-Claude Killy won his three gold medals in Grenoble, he was skiing on leather clip boots – but with a difference. His boots were higher in the back, and reinforced with fibreglass. Even with these improvements, Killy still changed his boots every month or so to make sure they were always as supporting as possible.

Nowadays, modern boots retain their strength and support for a long time. A favourite pair of Lange boots I had during my last three seasons became virtually my only pair of boots. They were so comfortable and race-effective that I didn't want to ski in anything else. Because they worked for me I turned down offers from other boot manufacturers to ski in their products, and I treated those Langes like old friends. When I finally hung them up at Lake Louise they still had as much life in them as when they started.

The boot companies have, over the years, been just as active as the ski manufacturers in trying out new systems. In 1971 Willy Bailey was successful in getting me fitted for a, then revolutionary, pair of plastic-coated leather, foam-injection boots, made by a firm called Molitor. I had to stand on a bench while they pumped hot gunge into the boot to conform to the shape of my foot. It was agony – a little like having hot concrete setting around your foot. All the blood flow was cut off, and I nearly passed out as I waited for the flow material to harden. When it did, I have to say that it worked. Those boots fitted perfectly and they were good to ski on but, at the end of the season another manufacturer, Henke, offered to supply me with boots for nothing. So, despite the comfort of the Molitors, I switched to Henke: they were not so comfortable.

The new boots, like the Molitors, were plastic-coated leather but when new were so stiff that I could hardly get my feet into them. To make matters worse I had suffered some sunburn to the tops of my feet just before, and the sheer effort of forcing my feet into the boots was torture. However, although virtually rigid when new, they became as soft as tennis shoes by the time they had been skied on for a while. This, of course, was totally unsatisfactory and I arranged a deal with Kastinger. It was an association that was to last up until 1977 when I became involved with Salomon.

Salomon had been manufacturing ski bindings for many years but in the mid-seventies decided to diversify into ski boots. The company had always been associated with the racing side of the business and they were keen to put a boot suitable for competition on the market. Most racers on the circuit had heard rumours that this development was taking place and some had seen prototypes, but it wasn't until the summer of 1977 that I found myself amongst a group of racers at Val Thorens to test the revolutionary new boot.

I was impressed with it and its unusual design philosophy, but felt that some changes needed to be made if it was to be suitable for downhill racing. Salomon, of course, wanted the boot used for downhill, and asked me if I would help develop it by using it in competition. I agreed, and became the first racer on the World Cup circuit regularly skiing on Salomon.

The boot we had tried out at Val Thorens reacted too precisely for downhill – a characteristic that made it unsuitable for the subtle changes in terrain encountered in that event – and work had to be done to make it somewhat more forgiving.

Various things were tried. The boot was lowered slightly and different materials were used in the cuff and in the composition of the outside shell. It was quite an exciting time for me, for I appreciated being involved in the development of something new from the ground up. It was much more satisfying having a relationship with a company that required participation in product development rather than just being given a pair of established boots and told to ski in them.

It is unfortunate that, in spite of all the development work, the Salomon design never became the perfect racing boot we all hoped it would be. Various elements proved extremely difficult to get just right and, eventually, I had to sever my connection with the company.

In New Zealand I did alternate testing runs on Salomon and Lange boots, and then used Lange in my first race there. I won the race and naturally became quite keen on the boot. I felt it adapted itself to downhill better than Salomon, and was of more assistance in my quest for those elusive tenths of a second that mean the difference between success and failure. I was still happy to continue with Salomon bindings, but I felt I couldn't continue to take a gamble on a boot I suspected wasn't quite race-fit. I needed results too badly to do that.

So, skis and boots were changing all the time – but what of bindings? No piece of skiing equipment has changed more radically than these fundamental devices over the years. The first downhillers strapped their skis to their boots with leather straps but, after World War II, safety bindings based on springs and tension release began to appear. In essence, all bindings attempt to keep you on your skis when you are doing what you want and release you as soon as something radical goes wrong. By and large all the major binding manufacturers have been successful in this and it is rare, provided the binding has been properly mounted and adjusted, for skiers to crash through binding failure. In my own case it has happened just once – the time a binding pre-released on a bump and the flying loose ski cut into my leg – and I have had very little cause for complaint from any binding I have used.

In the very early days I started on Look Nevada and had a brief spell on Gertsch before taking up with Salomon in the Three Musketeer days. It is somehow ironic that, for my last year of racing,

I should switch back to Look. Yet another completion of a Bartelski full circle.

Of course bindings are mechanical devices and need constant checking. In this respect all the companies, and particularly Look in my last year, have done a great job. A representative of the company was at each start wiping the snow from the boots and checking that the binding was functioning correctly; it was a final safety check that I always appreciated.

The benefits of painstaking research into bindings at the racing level has been felt at the recreational level perhaps more than anywhere. Today orthopaedic surgeons have to set far fewer broken legs than they did only about ten years ago. Bindings are now very sophisticated and reliable, and the know-how behind adjusting the spring setting for different standards and weights of skier has improved with every new technological development. Skiers will always fall, of course, but these days the likelihood is more for a sore shoulder or head than a broken leg.

For a downhill racer the biggest force he has to contend with is the air. At average speeds of 65 to 70mph the force of the wind on the body is like a brake, and the racer has to find ways of cutting down wind resistance to increase speed. A fundamental way of doing this is to adopt the most effective crouch position – but just what *is* the most effective position? The only way it was possible to find out was by using wind tunnels and checking the flow of fast-moving air over the body. I first used a wind tunnel with Robin Bailey in 1975 and have used them since as a way of fine-tuning my position in the tuck. It is surprising how a tiny change in the body's position can make a major change in the way the air flows. Too many eddies behind the body have the effect of sucking the skier back, but with a few adjustments to the positions of the arms and head, many of these eddies can be eliminated. That can make all the difference to the time on a fast *schuss*.

It was the Italians, and Erwin Stricker in particular, who first really researched aerodynamics as a way of increasing downhill speed. As early as 1972 they started using skin-tight plastic suits for their skiing. None of them was skiing well, in fact some were downright slapdash, but their times were remarkable. It was some time before it was realised that the suits were largely responsible.

In 1975 the Germans came up with an all-white, skin-tight and air-tight racing suit that also completely covered the boots. It was fantastically smart – the racers looked as though they could cut through the air like a knife. However they only used these suits for races, never for training, a fact that nearly caught one of their own racers unawares. Michel Wieth had practised in his ordinary suit at Val d'Isère in 1975 and then came a surprising third in the actual race. However, in an interview afterwards, he said that he was cutting through the air so cleanly, and so much faster than he had in training, that he could hardly keep on the track.

Tests showed that the plastic suits were a full three seconds faster than the ordinary suits we had been using that let air through; but they had one major disadvantage. If you managed to stay upright from top to bottom of a downhill, the plastic suit got you there quicker – but if you fell, there was nothing to stop you. There was negligible friction between the suit and the snow and racers were finding it virtually impossible to stop in a fall. This meant, of course, that racers were sliding into trees and other obstacles and were doing themselves more damage than would otherwise be the case.

After some deliberation the authorities felt they could not allow the suits to continue in use, and ruled that plastic could only be used if it was an inside material with a rougher, textured, material on the outside. They required this new type to be used from the beginning of 1976.

The new suits were still quicker than the pre-plastic ones but, after a time, complaints started coming in from the racers. The suits were fine when worn with anoraks and trousers over the top before a race but, as soon as the outer garments were discarded after the final warm-up, the sweat built up inside them cooled. As the inside material was impermeable, sweat had no way of evaporating, and several skiers were complaining of trouble with their backs as a result.

Obviously the authorities had to think again and this time, at the end of 1977, they came up with a standard for downhill suits. From that time on, suits had to be able to let through a given quantity of air under a given pressure. All of them had to be tested and were required to be inside the limits set.

Frantic activity began in the laboratories of ski-suit manufacturers. Descente came up with a material that just about matched the legal limit, so they stole a march on the competition – but the others were not giving up.

At a race in Morzine in January 1979 Ken Read won in a suit that had not been tested. After the race the officials required this to be done, and when it was found that the suit did not let the required amount of air through, Ken was disqualified. This was a pity as even Karl Kahr, the Austrian coach, had said that he would have won the race anyway – but the officials' attitude was that rules were rules, and they were there to be obeyed.

Even with the new regulations, however, the problem of suits refused to go away. In 1978–79 the Austrians were not doing too well and Atomic asked me to go and test their suits against the Italian ones I was using. In the tests it was consistently shown that the Italian suits were two-tenths of a second faster over a thirty-second run. This was at the fairly slow speed of 55mph and represented something like a second over a full downhill course. Not surprisingly, the Austrians turned up at the next race sporting new Japanese suits.

Today the research and the battle still goes on. All the companies are looking for faster suits that still meet the criteria set by FIS. It is a game of one-upmanship that will go on as long as there is ski racing.

Ski and equipment testing, although mostly boring, can have its lighter moments. My own testing was done at the MIRA wind tunnel in Nuneaton, where almost everything can be simulated – from conditions for trucks and racing cars to the upward forces a skier creates with his own body at speed. After my fall on to a tree stump before the 1982 Val Gardena race, the guys at MIRA sent me a telegram saying: 'Sorry unable to simulate tree-stumps. Get well soon.' It was one of those little things that makes all the effort and hard work put into a sport worthwhile.

As a final word about equipment in general it is fair to say that every racer is trying all the time to get that little extra edge for himself. Some will try aerodynamically-designed full-face helmets (although most have found these too cumbersome). Some will try wearing no clothes under their suits, while others will trim down the tips of their skis so they do not protrude up and catch the wind too much. The effect of most of these little refinements is more psychological than practical, but who is to say how important or not the psychological is in winning ski races? The only one of the more minor developments that all racers have adopted is the bent racing ski pole. These were developed to allow the racer to keep his poles out of the way in a tuck, and to let him keep his hands and elbows in out of the airstream.

Other than these tiny modifications, there is little that can be done now radically to change downhill racing. The rules are so tight that only minute changes can be made to equipment if it is to stay within the rules and, unless something totally unexpected happens, downhilling will stay pretty much as it is today.

The only person who really made any serious attempt to change the system was the Austrian, Werner 'the Grisly' Grissman. In practice for the World Cup in St Anton during February 1981 Werner came down the hill with rockets strapped to his waist. About five hundred metres from the finish he attempted to light them. He failed, but had he done so he would have given finishing a totally new dimension . . .

Werner's little joke had everyone in fits, but there was a more serious side to it. He had devised his little bit of drama to hide the fact that he was trying out a different make of boot to the ones he was under contract to wear. His team found out and the management felt it was a sufficiently serious infringement of Ski Pool regulations for him to be suspended from the team. Nevertheless I will always remember Werner's attempt at rocket-powered descent. Who knows, maybe one day he will be considered the father of a completely new sport!

— 8 —
LIFE ON THE
ROAD

Around 1976, Englishman Rick Gunnel asked the authorities in Kitzbühel for permission to set up an English pub in the town. This request was granted immediately – the Austrians did not believe that such a pub could survive more than a couple of months – and he was given a licence until four am. Needless to say Rick not only survived, he prospered. Indeed, he prospered so much that the good burghers of Kitzbühel felt compelled to revoke his four am licence and limit him to midnight closing. It is also hardly necessary to say that Rick's pub, suitably called *The Londoner*, became a favourite with members of the British ski team. After the Kitzbühel race we would always congregate there to let off steam before moving on to the next location.

At one of these unwinding sessions, in 1980, Rick suggested inviting all the others on the circuit to an English-style party. No sooner was this suggested than it was done. Most of the older guys came down – Ken Read, Steve Podborski, Harti Weirather, Andy Mill, Franz Klammer, Michel Weith, to name but a few. Bottles of champagne, courtesy of Rick, were thrust in their hands as they came through the door.

It was a great party. There were scenes of such devilry and drunkenness that to tell them all would require a book in itself – and anyway this book is intended for family entertainment! Suffice it to say that more champagne ended up on the floor than down the throats of the revellers. The event was such a success that it was decided to hold one annually: it was to be Britain's great contribution to downhill ski racing.

After word got around, the annual *Londoner* party became *the* social event of the circuit. More people tried to get in than could be accommodated, and the ones we did let in crowded the place to such an extent that it was sometimes necessary to pass bodies out over the heads of everyone else.

Always there was a queue of people at the door trying to get in and our technique was to go and look, one at a time, and let in those we knew, along with the prettiest of the others. Once in, however, it was up to each person to survive. Ice buckets, spilling their contents as they went, constantly travelled upside down the length of the bar, and quite often I found myself doing the near-impossible – drinking one bottle of champagne, pouring another over somebody's head, and squirting another that had been shaken up into some victim's face. Such a feat would normally require three arms, but somehow I managed it – it was that sort of party. Spirits were so high that the impossible was possible.

At the 1982 party James Hunt was a guest, and he enjoyed it so much he immediately wanted to know how to go about becoming a ski racer. I had to tell him that other resorts didn't offer such a party. Kitzbühel, I told him, was our equivalent of the Monaco Grand Prix – quite definitely a one-off in the season.

In 1983, my last year as a racer, the party was the biggest ever. As well as all the regulars, most of the younger racers came along, as did Nelson Piquet and his girlfriend and the German racing driver, Manfred Winkelhock. The Canadian and American ski teams were there in force (the Canadians, conveniently, always contrived to win the race, ensuring the party of a lively, victory-celebrating mood); and two British press representatives, David Vine and John Samuel, were allowed in provided that anything they saw was totally off the record!

Over two hundred bottles of champagne were consumed, or spilled, during the evening and, when it came to clearing up there was more broken glass than glass left intact, or at least so it seemed. When the champagne finally ran out – as it was bound to do at the rate we were disposing of it – I started filling my friends' glasses with beer. Anyone else who asked for a beer got one in the face – not very sociable I'll admit, but hilarious fun!

The party didn't finish until the very early hours of the morning and finally there was time for a quick, reviving shower in the hotel before driving down to Ljubjana for the Yugoslavian internal flight we were all booked on to take us to the Olympic course trials at Sarajevo.

When we finally got onto the plane we were a sorry-looking group of skiers indeed. Pinched eyes tried hard to keep out the brilliant morning light, while dark glasses for those who had them were the order of the day. We certainly paid our dues for that party, but I, for one, wouldn't have had it any other way.

There are many stark contrasts on the circuit: that between the good-natured conviviality of our party and what we found in Yugoslavia was one of the starkest of all.

The hotel we were put in at Sarajevo was a huge, fourteen-storey tribute to the glory of Communism; I was on the eleventh floor. After what seemed like hours I finally fought my way to the front of a throng of angry racers, all trying to get their room numbers and general information, and found my way to the lift. There were only two in the hotel. When I finally found my home-from-home behind the Iron Curtain I was pleased to find I had a room to myself, but not so pleased with the room itself. To say it was barren would be praising it. There was nothing to look at and the view from the window reminded me of the smoky and dowdy Midlands towns of Industrial Revolution England. It was uninspiring to say the least.

As I was only going to be in Yugoslavia for five days, I was travelling light, without my usual cassette recorder, so my only entertainment seemed likely to be gazing out of the window at the smog. Fortunately I knew that Nick Phipps of the British bob team was in the town and I had just decided to go and look for him when he knocked on my door. Nick and I had been training together in the summer and it was good to have some friendly conversation, but that was the only good thing I found.

The skiing was forty-five minutes away by bus, and the only snow was on the course (shovelled there by Yugoslav Army conscripts). There was no snow for free skiing. There wasn't an English newspaper to be found in the town, and the food in the hotel was dreadful. No matter what it was called – ham, chicken or cheeseburger – it always managed to look and taste the same. Certainly there was no eager anticipation of meal times and, although I ate regularly, I still managed to lose four pounds in weight during the five days.

It was one of the most miserable places I had ever encountered in ten years on the World Cup circuit. The only character my room had came from the dirty clothes I scattered around it and the only pleasure I could look forward to each day was a 'phone call to my girlfriend in London. Those five days cost me a fortune in telephone calls, but without that daily link with the real world I could quite easily have gone round the twist.

Fortunately, life in general on the World Cup circuit was better than that.

During my early days on the circuit the season would begin every year at Val d'Isère, where there would be something of a carnival atmosphere in the air. Both the men and the girls would be racing in the resort and there was an excited atmosphere as we all greeted each other after the summer and chatted about our hopes and dreams for the new season. I often used to join the Canadian men and the German girls in the local coffee shop which was always a jovial meeting. It was a great way to start the season – we were all in it together, and no one yet had a success or a failure.

Unfortunately much of that has now ended. For the 1983 season the FIS World Cup committee scheduled a race at Laax to begin the season for the men, but it was cancelled through lack of snow and a race was held instead at Pontresina. When, finally, we got to Val d'Isère for the second race, the girls were just about to move off somewhere else and the coffee shop was dead.

The season seemed to lose much of its joy because of the re-arranged start and it is to be hoped that the organisers get back to the old system of starting everything off, boys and girls together, in Val d'Isère. Obviously skiing is a winter sport and dependent on the vagaries of the weather but, everything being equal, it would help to keep the camaraderie of the sport alive if the joint start could be revived.

Once on the road, the thing that tends to dominate life is the quality of the food. Whenever I found myself in a hotel that served good, appetising meals, I was able to put up with no English papers or the lack of a 'phone in my room. (For me, not having a 'phone on hand is a bit like hell on earth – but I have to admit that whenever I didn't have one, I was able to keep my costs right down. Being a bit of a telephone addict, if there was one I had to use it, a habit which had a disastrous effect on my bank balance!)

My favourite gastronomic stop-over was always the Hotel Laurin in Val Gardena. This small family hotel wasn't in the five-star league by any means, the rooms were of modest size and the only telephone was a booth in the foyer: but, ah, the food. Delicious home-made pasta and Austrian veal dishes were all cooked with care and served with style. Nowhere on the circuit looked after the inner man quite as well as the Laurin and, despite the fact that I had good and bad years on the Val Gardena course, I never discovered a mistake in any course served at the hotel's tables. Whenever I was there I always managed to put on a pound or two and it was fortunate that I never stayed more than six days at a stretch – otherwise I would have had to buy a whole new wardrobe.

At the other end of the gastronomic spectrum is, surprisingly, Aspen in the US Rockies. This wild, swinging ski town has perhaps more restaurants than any other ski resort in the world but – until the 1983 season anyway – these were not for the racers.

In Aspen all the racers stayed in a large hotel and ate at a self-service cafeteria. I can't say that the food was actually bad but having to queue for it and then find a table was a bit like being at boarding school, definitely not to my liking. For the 1983 season racers were allowed to try the restaurants of the town but only up to a certain cash limit, which meant that we had to restrict ourselves to the cheap end of the menu. Still, at least we got the friendliness of a restaurant atmosphere, which was a big improvement.

Nevertheless, Aspen has a special ambience not found anywhere else on the circuit. From the moment we flew in and saw the Lear jets lining the runway we knew we were in a place with a few bucks around. Indeed, the difference between the approach to World Cup racing in Aspen and World Cup racing in a European resort is comparable with the difference between a beach donkey and a Derby winner. In Europe they have become a bit blasé about the World Cup. The racers would arrive in the resort, the practices would be held, the race would go as planned (weather permitting) and everyone would leave. There would be no special pomp and circumstance, just work as usual on the circuit.

In America, however, they do things in style. At the beginning of the week the organisers would stage an opening ceremony. It wasn't exactly popular with most of the racers, and quite often the junior member of the team would be delegated to attend, but it typified the Aspen razzmatazz. During the week the town always put on a firework display of such magnificence that we less-affluent British skiers always felt the cost must be more than the entire British team's travelling budget!

Celebrity races were organised to enhance the carnival atmosphere, and film personalities would pack the town, emphasising its already trendy image. Going up in a chairlift one day I travelled with Britt Ekland (much to the chagrin of team ladies' man Koni Rupprechter) but I have to say I was rather disillusioned. Here was this luminary of the film world skiing in a jewel-encrusted watch and on skis with her name delicately engraved on each – not, I suspect, so that she could tell them from the skis of the hoi polloi, but rather that they realise they were encountering royalty. Not, I think, a lady of modest ego!

But Aspen is a fun place, and the best possible place to end the season. Most of the bars have a country-and-western band or singer and everyone wears stetsons (each racer is given a stetson every year, and I now have quite a collection gathering dust in London – they don't seem to go down too well in the City). The waitresses and barmaids, in typical American style, wear tiny, revealing uniforms – usually based loosely on some western motif – and everyone of course speaks English, a welcome relief for many of the skiers on the circuit.

In a nutshell, Aspen is a holiday town. It is a town that has virtually been created by skiers and, since vast numbers of Americans spend small fortunes on annual skiing holidays, there is no shortage of entertainments. It gave to the end of each season the same feelings of bonhomie that the early gatherings in Val d'Isère gave to the beginning. It is one of the places I shall miss most as I settle into my retirement.

One of the places I shall remember least is Morzine in the French Savoie. It is an uninspiring little town at the best of times but, for the last two seasons I went there, the boredom of the place was compounded by non-stop rain. Apart from that, Morzine offered very little in the way of extra-curricular activities. On the way there most people stopped off in Geneva to pick up whatever English newspapers and magazines were available – usually *Time* and *Newsweek* – to while away the lonely Morzine nights.

In my times there the only welcome breaks were a dinner the British boys were taken to by BBC men David Vine and Jim Reside, and an ice-skating session organised by the hockey-mad Canadians, who always travel with their boots in their bags. I must say I quite enjoyed those games on the ice but I certainly knew I had ankles the next day!

At the dinner with David Vine, Stuart Fitzsimmons asked Jim Reside, a fellow Scot and David's producer, if he could borrow the telephone in his room to call his girlfriend. After slight hesitation, Jim agreed, but this was nothing to the Scotsman's agitation as Stuart stayed away fifteen, thirty, forty-five minutes. Every two minutes or so Jim would look at his watch as he calculated the bill. When Stuart finally came back after threequarters of an hour, he had a smirk on his face while Jim's was considerably longer . . . nothing was actually said, but I didn't fancy Stuart's chances of ever getting another 'phone call out of Jim!

David Vine used to take us out to dinner about once every other race and, even after ten years on the circuit, they were highlights. It was wonderful not to have to worry about the bill and to be able to choose anything from the menu.

Circuit life, of course, is life on the road, and life on the road means travel; lots of it. In my two years with the Dutch, this was done in a tiny Lancia car. I remember one year when I was setting out from Val d'Isère to Wengen, I received a call from Bob Miller, a Canadian skiing friend who was stuck in Chamonix. With Mark Amis also in the car, I detoured to Chamonix to pick Bob up and bundled him and his gear in. It wasn't easy. The Lancia was essentially a two plus two, but we had twenty pairs of skis on the roof, a bulging boot and Mark squashed in the back nursing seven pairs of ski boots. When we arrived at Lauterbrunnen to catch the train that would take us up to car-less Wengen, the station staff couldn't believe the gear that seemed to issue endlessly from the car.

Once in Wengen, we found ourselves in one of those once-gracious, but now slightly decayed, Swiss hotels that creaked every time you took a step and transmitted the noise of a cassette player, even on low volume, to every corner of the building. With considerable pleasure we eventually (some years later) had ourselves transferred to the Park Hotel, where the American team also stayed. It was like coming out of some railway hotel in Britain and finding yourself in the Inn on the Park.

The management of the Park Hotel, at least after a change of management in 1981, was very agreeably disposed towards ski racers; something not very common in five-star hotels. They supplied us with fantastic buffet lunches of the stuff-yourself-till-you-burst type (not really recommended for someone who likes his food as much as I do) and they made special efforts to look after the unusual needs of the racers.

For the Lauberhorn race in Wengen the hotel would be humming with racers, pressmen, television crews and the like. It was always noisy and active. Often there were television cables snaking into the lounge as CBS or some other US network interviewed one of the Mahre twins and it couldn't have been an easy life for the ordinary tariff-paying guests of the hotel. Yet the management always succeeded in smoothing out any little ruffles before they developed and, if anything, the regular guests seemed to enjoy the special ambience that the white circus gave the hotel for the week. Certainly the racers appreciated the efforts made by everyone, management and guests alike.

Once I got back with the British team the travel between race venues was by team bus – more convenient in some ways than the cramped conditions of the car but a lot less comfortable. Whenever we were leaving somewhere I would have to pack up my twelve pairs of skis into bags and load them, along with the skis of the other members, into the back of the bus. By the time everything was in – skis, boots, slalom poles, personal baggage and the rest – it was packed to roof level. The team members would then cram into the front for the slow, shake, rattle and roll journey to the next race. They were boring trips and the monotony was relieved only by the frequent stops the old bus had to make for petrol. These gave us a chance to stretch our legs and down a quick cup of *capuccino*: a necessary energy supplement as, in bad weather, we often had to bounce up and down in the back to give the traction wheels some grip on the steep alpine passes.

The building of the Brenner pass, the Arlberg tunnel, the St Gotthard tunnel, the Inn motorway and the like made life much easier on these journeys in later years but, in the early days before they were built, just getting that van over the passes was a major achievement in itself.

When we were on the road, the circus nature of the World Cup circuit would really reveal itself. It wasn't just us on the road: every team, every trainer, every pressman, television crew and company equipment support man would be there as well. When we stopped for petrol or a bite to eat we would invariably find someone we knew there too. Our progress was exactly like any circus's – pulling down its gear in one town, taking to the road, and setting up again in another. It made us aware that, as well as being sportsmen, we were entertainers, and nowhere was this more apparent than in Kitzbühel.

Whenever we arrived there the town would already be buzzing with the crowds who had swarmed down from Munich for the race. Days before the teams arrived, the coat-racks in the Stamperl café would be drooping under the weight of fur coats and the requests for autographs were so frequent that they became annoying. Many of the racers would hide themselves away from this in the sanctuary of their hotels, but none of them really minded. The atmosphere of the town, of all the European venues, most closely approached the carnival atmosphere of Aspen. In Kitzbühel, as skiers and as entertainers, we felt we were appreciated. The tourists were happy to be on holiday and anticipating the excitement of a race, the shopkeepers were happy as they watched the money flowing into their cash registers, and the racers were happy that they were once again in a town that helped to make ski racing fun. For me, going to Kitzbühel was really going home; it was a high spot of the season.

But despite the festive atmosphere in the streets the very nature of modern, high-technology ski racing means that racers cannot let their hair down until the race is over. In the old days I used to watch the great racers – Killy, Schranz, Mauduit *et al* – come off the slopes at the end of the day to be entertained at tea-dances by the café owners. The public would pack in, to ogle the stars sitting at tables adorned with their national flags, while the racers would put in the groundwork chatting-up of ladies in preparation for the more serious entertainment later in the evening. Once I saw Karl Schranz huddled together with Jochen Rindt – my two heroes together at the same time: almost too much for a young heart to bear.

In those days the racers had a very full social life for the whole week, but these days it is impossible. Not too long ago Werner Grissman complained to me that racers were not like they used to be.

Instead of working hard and playing hard every day, they were working hard for five days and saving up the high jinks for Saturday night. Werner complained that, instead of seeing racers enjoy themselves at tea-dances, all he could see was young men in tracksuits pounding the beat seriously with their trainers in the build-up to the race. In some ways I have to agree with him. Ski racing *is* more serious than it used to be – but then so is motor racing. As technology improves and the rewards of success (to the companies, not the racers) become greater, so the pressure on the racer to apply himself totally to the job in hand become greater.

I myself felt the pressure so strongly that I had to closet myself away from all the festivities and concentrate on nothing but the race on the Saturday. Once that was over, of course, life became a different kettle of fish: then it was time for the *Londoner* party and uninhibited revels.

Occasionally on the circuit there would be a break in the programme of two or three days and, when these came, we were at a loose end. They presented a real problem to the British, Canadians and Americans. The Austrians, Swiss and French could just go home for those days, get their washing done, catch up on their mail and generally relax. We could not do that since the costs would have been prohibitive. We couldn't even stay in the resort. Most of the race centres on the circuit were only too happy to see you at the beginning of the week and were happy to play host until the race was over – but, as soon as it was, we had to leave. There was no leeway, the hospitality was over and we had to hit the road. This used to annoy me considerably. If the resorts had been a bit more flexible and let us stay on for these little holidays there would have been no problems for us but, as the generosity dried up with a rush on Sunday morning, we were left in an embarrassing vacuum.

During the Robin Bailey days things were not so difficult. He was a member of the Alpbach Visitors Ski Club, and used to arrange for us to stay with Billy and Dinny Paterson who ran the club. The scope of their hospitality was enormous and we had a real home from home. Evenings spent in the local *keller* – which, although the village was tiny, had more stunningly beautiful girls per square inch than almost any other nightspot in Europe – were always great fun. I remember one night Willy won his first trophy there: the 'Mr

Alpbach' title. He was supposed to sing a couple of songs to the strumming of his own guitar and flex his muscles a little with his shirt off. Unfortunately Willy's guitar playing was of interest only to alley cats, but he made up for this with a comic routine that had the locals rolling in the aisles. He thoroughly deserved his title.

Even when Robin Bailey had gone, the Alpbach Visitors Club continued to make us welcome and we went there several times. Mostly, though, we would head for Geneva for a bit of city life. In theory the Federation would meet our expenses during the breaks but it never quite worked out that way. Receipts that we submitted were often disputed and we were required to nourish ourselves on £2 at lunch and just over £3 for dinner – this in the inflation-racked Europe of 1983!

But even though we were forced to spend some of our own money on these breaks they were worth it. In Geneva we were away from the mountains and snow and would be able to enjoy films and a side of life missing in the van-and-suitcase style of life on the road. It wasn't the same as the total relaxation the Europeans could get in their own homes, and thus we were at an obvious disadvantage, but we made as much of the rest as we could.

Of all the team members I was the luckiest in that I did, for the last five years of my career anyway, have a European home to go to. Many breaks would be spent with my parents in Zell am See. My usual habit would be to drive up and immediately grab the *Autosport* magazines to catch up on what had been going on. My interest was such that my parents knew better than to attempt to talk to me until the magazines had been read from cover to cover. During dinner I would regale them with the news from the circuit, but the rest of the time would normally be spent analysing videos over and over again as I planned my attack for the next race.

Basically, the pattern of the circuit was travel, train, race . . . travel, train, race. Sometimes a party would be thrown in for relief but the sheer routine of road life was enervating. When everything packed up after Aspen few people were not looking forward to the more relaxed change of pace that came with the summer.

— 9 —
SOME
PERSONALITIES

There's an old adage in downhill racing that this week's winner is next week's also-ran. To some extent it is true; certainly skiers do not win with the consistency of track athletes. But there are people in our sport who have won much more consistently than others. Harti Weirather, Peter Müller, Ken Read, Steve Podborski and, perhaps most of all, Franz Klammer, are names that the public associate with the winner's podium. Of these, perhaps the most interesting is the old man of the game, Franz Klammer (one year older than me).

A farm boy from Corinthia in southern Austria, Franz took to ski racing as naturally as an English boy would take to playing football in the street. He had his early troubles rising through the multitude of young hopefuls that Austria spawns every year but, when I first met him at a Europa Cup race in 1972, he pulled out all the stops for the first time and took his soon customary position on the top of the rostrum. In those days I only bumped into him every so often riding up chairlifts – he was just another guy on the circuit. But as time passed I got to know him better. Just prior to the World Championships at Garmisch in 1978 I asked him if he was going to retire after the race and do promotional work, and perhaps professional racing, in the United States. Several rumours had been buzzing around, both on the circuit and in the press, that this was the case.

But he scotched those rumours abruptly.

'Sure', he said, 'I'm interested, but I couldn't see myself ever giving up so that I could only watch other people doing what I like doing best. The most enjoyable thing in my life is skiing these classic downhill courses. If I did anything else I would have to stop doing that and that's something I couldn't even think about.'

Klammer got a lot of stick for his decision not to retire. He didn't win the World Championships – he was going through a lean spell, and the Austrian press showed him no mercy. They said he was past it and that he had lost his nerve after his younger brother became a paraplegic following a downhill crash.

It always annoyed me that Klammer had to put up with that kind of baiting. He was just doing what he wanted to do. Okay, so he wasn't winning, but ski racing isn't just winning. Winning is the jam when it comes, but if everyone called it a day when they weren't winning or had struck a loss of form there would be very few people left to ski World Cup downhills.

Like most racers, Klammer was having his share of problems over equipment but he persevered and slowly fought his way back. For a long time he was so intense about his skiing, and was trying so hard, that he got slower and slower – but he stuck at it, tidied up his style, had a break on the equipment front and astounded the world with his great comeback win at Val d'Isère in December 1981. It was a wonderful reward for a man who had been written off by his own country, a tribute to a great fighting spirit. To go on and take the 1982–83 World Cup downhill championship – something even he didn't think was really on – says all there is to say about the tenaciousness of the man. He didn't think about his age (neither did I really – it's only the press that do) and he carried on where weaker men would have wilted. No lover of ski racing and certainly no racer begrudged him that championship. He has put a tremendous amount into the sport, and he deserved to take a little out.

Franz used to come to our parties in *The Londoner* at Kitzbühel, but I never really got to know him until I got into the first group myself. That was because first-groupers as a whole don't really look back to see who is coming up, so Franz and I could only really see each other – in the figurative sense – when we were both in that élite group. Even so, although we often started before or after each other, I never really had a long talk with the Austrian until after the last race in Aspen. A party had been thrown by Ulli Forster, a wealthy friend of the Austrian team, and the champagne was flowing. Tongues were loosened and people who had skied against each other all season began to talk to each other without inhibition for the first time.

I found myself in a corner talking to Franz and he raised the matter of the Val Gardena race. It turned out that my second placing had annoyed him. He had won at Val d'Isère the week before and he reckoned he had skied well enough at Val Gardena to be in the frame. When I came down and beat him he couldn't believe it.

'It really brassed me off', he said, 'watching some damned Englishman – someone I regarded as a tourist on the circuit – beating my time. I suspected it was a fluke – you had only been in the twenties until then and yet managed to beat me.'

I found his attitude very difficult to swallow. I had made more sacrifices to reach that position than he had ever made in getting to where he was. It was annoying that he had no idea of the problems we faced or the efforts we had put in to get amongst the leaders. I didn't let him stay ignorant for long.

It turned out that although he had regarded my Val Gardena result as a fluke, he had changed his mind after my skiing over the rest of that season. He said the results proved I was a worthy first-fifteen skier, and virtually welcomed me into the 'brotherhood'. Obviously I was pleased that my efforts had commanded some respect from him, but I was more pleased that I had had an opportunity to put him in the picture about the realities of British skiing.

Of all the people in the 'inner sanctum' of the first fifteen, one of the nicest was Harti Weirather. As well as being a fantastically accomplished technical skier, Harti was a genuine lover of the sport. Many a time we put our heads together during summer breaks to try to work out ways of improving ski racing.

Harti's view was that the whole system was crazy. Here we are, he said to me once, training and taking the risks, while all the money goes to the ski pool which is training the juniors who will replace us. I couldn't have agreed with him more.

Although they were team-mates and had a public respect for each other, Harti and Franz were not the best of mates. This was more than just professional rivalry – indeed I am sure that it was as rivals that they valued each other most – and it is more likely that their different backgrounds were the root cause. Harti had won a scholarship to Stams (virtually the academy of Austrian ski racing) and this didn't go down too well with Klammer's more down-to-earth mentality. Their differences were a sort of variation on the university versus the 'university of life' approach to the world.

The 1982 World Championships at Schladming were Harti's greatest personal triumph. In training he had been doing nothing, and I remember seeing him shaking his head with one of the Austrian downhill coaches, totally exasperated because he couldn't put his finger on what was wrong and where he could pick up some time.

We were on a course inspection, and as I passed Harti and his coach on a corner he shook his head at me too.

'It's crazy, it's crazy', he said. 'I don't know what I'm going to do in the race tomorrow.'

Like me, however, Harti wasn't a training skier – he could never find his best in training sessions. On race day it was different. The man who had been shaking his head in frustration the day before found a completely unsuspected gear. He flew that course like a demon, and this coupled with his superb technique took him to the victor's laurels.

Down in the finish area he came up to me again. 'It's crazy, it's crazy', were again the words on his lips. He didn't know where he had picked up those elusive fractions of speed but he didn't really care. He had won.

After the race we were invited to dinner with Ulli Forster (the Swiss lady who had thrown the party at Aspen during which I had had my talk with Klammer) and a German businessman was also there. Harti decided to air his views about the way the World Cup system should be changed, about how shamateurism should be ended, and things brought out into the open with racers getting paid as professionals for their efforts – just as Grand Prix drivers did. The conversation lasted until three in the morning, and some useful ideas were tossed about as to how such changes could be achieved. The businessman seemed to be as keen as we were to do something about the situation; unfortunately, he never followed up his promises and another opportunity to initiate change was lost.

It has to be remembered when thinking about Harti's plea for more direct payments to racers that, if he had been a top Grand Prix driver instead of a top downhiller, he would have been a rich man. He would have taken about the same risks but would have been compensated adequately for it. He loved ski racing and didn't want to stop, but it rankled that he was taking the risks for peanuts.

Another guy who felt deeply that the management of the sport should be changed was Peter Müller. I had known Peter since 1975 and was one of the few people on the circuit to like him. He was always at odds with his team-mates and his coaches (and I have to say that, had I been on a team with him, I might have found him a bit trying too) so he was something of a joke with the other racers. But Peter was very intense about his racing. He wished for nothing more than to win; that was what he was in the business for. He was an extremely argumentative man and, on one celebrated occasion, told his ski technician that he would never ski on a particular pair of skis again. Peter thought they were chronic bad runners and would have nothing to do with them. The serviceman said okay, and gave the skis to the Italian racer, Daniello Spardelotto, for the race at Val d'Isère. In the event Daniello raced those skis into third place, a fantastic result for him, with Peter one place behind, fourth. This incident did nothing for Peter's reputation amongst the other racers, in fact it reinforced his position as a figure of fun.

In my experience, though, Peter had his heart in the right place. He was always friendly to me, and it was he, for instance, who first congratulated me after my result at Val Gardena. He was a great bear of a man and would hug you in genuine delight for your success but, if you didn't watch it, that hug could be crippling – especially if you were still struggling for breath after a race!

If he was anything, Peter Müller was the misunderstood man of the circuit. He wanted to win so desperately that he tended to have rows with his team and his coaches when things went wrong. He also wanted desperately to be popular, and for some reason was always unable to achieve the two.

If there was a man who was deservedly unpopular on the circuit, it was Leonard Stock. Stock had won the Olympic title at Lake Placid against the odds and become an instant hero in his home part of Austria. He never seemed able to handle that success, and he became a sort of school bully, always loud-mouthed and ill-mannered. If anyone was barging his way into the cable car, it was likely to be Stock. Once, when I was collecting some lift-passes for the British team from the cable car office at Diavolezza, Stock leaned over and grabbed one, saying 'I'll have one of those'. Such behaviour was typical of the man; it was one of the reasons he was quite generally disliked.

If Stock was perhaps the pariah, Steve Podborski, in the manner of an American high school, was the man voted Most Likely To Succeed. He was the 'Gentleman Jim' of the circus and never had a bad word to say about anyone. To see him and Harti Weirather congratulating each other after one of them had just beaten the other you would have thought they were on the same team instead of rivals. Steve's attitude was always 'try as hard as you can and if you get beaten you get beaten'. As long as he was satisfied he had done his best, he didn't resent the success of anyone else. That's a healthy attitude in ski racing, and one that some others would have done well to adopt.

Although Steve was as keen to win as anyone else, somehow it never seemed to dominate his thinking and he didn't allow himself to get 'hung up' by it. On one occasion when I was really low at the bottom of Sarajevo after a training run, my head in my hands with depression, it was Steve Podborski, and only Steve Podborski out of eighty-odd racers, who took the trouble to come up to me and say, 'Come on, it can't be that bad.' When most racers come down from training, they have thoughts only for themselves and their own performance. Podborski was different, and I appreciated his attempt to buck me up very much.

Podborski was to the Canadians what Harti Weirather was to the Austrians: both were thoroughly nice people with a remarkable gift for the technical side of ski racing. In the company of either of them the World Cup circuit was a pleasure. But despite being relatively quiet men for the world of downhilling, both Weirather and Podborski would have been considered positively boisterous in comparison with Ingemar Stenmark.

Most slalomers are quieter men than downhillers, but Ingemar took quietness to the 'nth' degree. To a large extent this was because his phenomenal success had made him into a living legend, so hounded by the press that he had to hide himself away in order to have any life of his own. But a lot of it, too, was in his own nature. Stenmark was not a man given to outward display. Until quite recently he would show no emotion at all in the finish area of his races, and he had never been a man to join others in a bar for a few beers and a chat. Consequently the Swede had a reputation for being aloof and stand-offish, but to me he was just a successful man in his chosen field who happened to have a different personality to those around him.

Certainly Stenmark would not see the press except at properly organised press conferences – but this was not because he scorned newsmen, rather because if he didn't see them all at once he would be pestered so much that he wouldn't have a moment's peace. It even got to the stage where, in order to get some privacy, he would only travel in a chairlift with his girlfriend – something no other racer I know of would dream of doing.

That Stenmark was a difficult man to get along with was unquestioned but he had not, as some people suggested, locked himself away in a castle, removed from the rest of the world. He recognised that he had a responsibility to put something back into the sport that had given him so much. He took no persuading, for instance, to come to England to give out the prizes at the All England Plastic Ski Slope Championships in May 1982. He didn't smile much at the prize-giving, and there were more silences during the dinner that followed than might otherwise have been the case, but he did come. He made the effort and many of the kids who competed in those races will be spurred on just because he was there to watch them.

An indication that Ingemar didn't consciously attempt to put people down comes from the fact that Stig Strand, another Swedish slalomer from the same village as Stenmark, sometimes saw him as something of a foreigner. Stenmark was just one of the world's loners and his insistence that he be left alone should have been respected. He gave enough pleasure to deserve that, at least.

Ingemar's main rival for slalom and giant slalom honours, American Phil Mahre, was also a quiet man, if not quite the loner that Stenmark had become. Phil, like his twin brother, Steve, for that matter, was a down-home, all-American boy who had brought Mom and apple pie into international ski racing. Both travelled the circuit with their wives and kids in tow, and for Phil to win the overall World Cup while looking after his wife and children at the same time was no mean achievement.

Skiing for the Mahres was just a winter sport – when they got home to Washington State at the end of the season they forgot about skiing completely. They rode their motorbikes, built their houses, took their kids on trips and became part of their local community again.

They didn't even bother about scheduled training programmes during the summer break. For them it was a case of forgetting skiing altogether and doing something completely different. That they could do this was a measure of just how gifted they were as athletes. Not just anybody could have got away with it – at least I hope that is the case, otherwise I have been doing an awful lot of very unpleasant work for nothing!

Once on the snow, however, both Mahres showed absolute dedication to what they were doing. Indeed Phil, who undertook all three disciplines, spent most of his time training and testing. But the man had such natural talent it sometimes took your breath away. On the first downhill training run at St Anton in the 1983 season, Phil skied the course and, when he got to the kangaroo jump near the bottom, casually did a full 360-degree helicopter turn in the air. It was a gesture of pure *joie de vivre* – he was enjoying his skiing and telling the world just that. He didn't do it to show off (I'm not sure he would know what that meant), rather it was the equivalent of the little whoop of joy sometimes given by people who are having a really good time in deep, light powder. It was the sign of a man who enjoyed his work.

Being twins, and identical twins at that, the Americans were a team within a team. Each knew exactly what the other wanted, and when they were speaking on the radio there was a rapport that no racer/trainer relationship could ever hope to match. It was uncanny sometimes. I have seen these guys, so alike to look at that it was almost impossible to tell them apart, come down a course one after the other and record times to within hundredths of a second of each other. It was almost as though they were thinking inside each other's heads.

Perhaps the best way of summing up the refreshing approach of these twins to ski racing came when Steve won the World Championship giant slalom. At the end of the race he pointed to his skis – not to advertise his manufacturer but to draw attention to a piece of sticky tape bearing the word 'Ginger'. This was the name of a daughter who had just been born and he was telling the world that he had done it for her. It wasn't dramatics, just a simple statement of fact.

Of all the people of the circuit, the one I got on with the best and whom I can most sincerely call a friend is Ken Read. Ken, of course, had a connection with us right back to the Musketeer days and our relationship had always been close, but as the years wore on that friendship got closer and closer. Naturally I was often envious of him because he was achieving what I had always dreamed of doing but, at the same time, his successes encouraged me because I knew there wasn't a great deal separating us: after all, I beat him in New Zealand and if I could do it there I could do it anywhere.

The thing that made Ken a success was sheer hard work. When he met me in Singapore before we travelled down to New Zealand Ken arranged a run in the park. It was humid to about one hundred per cent and I can't say I enjoyed it. I don't enjoy running even when conditions are perfect. I would have been happier on a bicycle, but Ken loved running and he arranged the programme. Typically, it was detailed and thorough. Ken always showed a dedicated and systematic approach to all his work. He was keen to do well and he knew that he could only achieve his goals if he was fit. Never in all the time I knew him did he deviate from this principle. Just on the work he put in he deserved his successes, and his example was an encouragement to me to keep going.

Ken had had his own troubles with his Federation and there were plenty of times when we sat together moping about our respective confrontations. He knew what it was like to hit his head against a brick wall just as well as I did – the only difference being that when he had his row, they fired the coach and not him!

Ken shared my conviction that much needed to be done to clean up and reorganise ski racing, and he was always prepared to air his views, a habit that didn't endear him to his own coaches or even those of other teams.

Ken epitomised the days of the Crazy Canucks. Even in training he always seemed to be going flat out, as though that was the only speed he knew, and his commitment and derring-do brought the best out of the other racers. I for one would have found life much harder on the World Cup circuit if Ken Read hadn't been around.

In the bus from Aspen to Denver on the journey to Lake Louise for the last race of 1983, Ken told me he was going to retire after it. I was surprised. I had already subconsciously made my own decision to retire, and I had never thought of Ken doing the same. We were approximately the same age, we had been in skiing about the same time and we were retiring after the same race. The only difference was that he was at the top and I was at the bottom.

The reasons for our respective retirements were thus more or less the same, but when Ken announced his decision publicly Canada gave him a fitting tribute. There was a banner headline and portrait on the front of the *Calgary Sun* but the last, acid, word had to come, typically, from Canada's trainer, John Ritchie. Ritchie was retiring himself and in an interview with the press said he could understand Ken's retirement.

'Ken is no longer Canada's number one – he is only Canada's number three.'

It was the sort of comment that could only have come from a trainer and said, more eloquently than we could, all there was to say about the rifts and animosities between coaches and racers.

Without Ken I doubt that Canada would have reached the peaks it did or have stamped its mark on world skiing. Ritchie's comment was certainly a justification of Ken's decision to retire.

TWO OF THE BEST
AND A HO-HUM

Of all the courses on the circuit the Hahnenkamm at Kitzbühel is easily my favourite. Right from the starting-gate this classic course doesn't let a racer relax for a mini-second; it requires total concentration from top to bottom.

Just standing in the gate at Kitzbühel is an experience in itself. All that can be seen is about forty yards to a blind, left-hand bend that you know leads into a chasm. In the old days this short start-run used to be very narrow, but in recent years some trees have been chopped down to make it slightly wider. Even so the run to the turn is still full of apprehension. No sooner have you negotiated the turn itself, at about 40mph, than you are falling away into the abyss of the Mausfalle at 70mph. The acceleration is fantastic – again using the overworked analogy with motor racing, a bit like an Indianapolis car; the 30mph gain is so quick it takes your breath away.

At the bottom of the Mausfalle, on what is usually quite rutted, hard-packed snow, the racer takes a left-hander, struggling all the time to keep up his speed. The turn has come at you in a rush, there was no time to set yourself up for it, but if you don't get it right the race can be over for you right here. Many an attempt at the Hahnenkamm has ended in a shower of snow at the bottom of the Mausfalle.

It is absolutely essential to be properly prepared for the 180-degree right-hander into the Steilhang. The G forces and the centrifugal pull involved in this turn are tremendous; they are literally trying to pull you off the course. To do it right you must be on the right line and have your body properly balanced. But the compression effect at the base of the Mausfalle – the tendency for the knees to get sucked violently into the body as it absorbs the transition from the very steep to the almost flat – tends to throw your weight over the back of the skis and, if this isn't rectified quickly, not an easy thing to do, the line and the balance into the Steilhang turn is already lost.

Even if everything is all right there is no time to congratulate yourself. No sooner are you clear of that than there is a left-hand knoll onto the cliff-like steepness of the Steilhang itself. Again, centrifugal forces are trying to pull you across the slope but your job is to go down it. Going across it loses time, but so does hard-edging as a way of countering the forces. It is one of the most crucial turns on the course. Ideally you have to be absolutely on line and as close to the fence as possible so that you can time your exit. Take it too early and you hit another knoll that can throw you into the nets, take it too late and you are in the nets anyway – and all this on sheet ice! This part of the course requires considerable subtlety. The more times you have skied it the better you can be, so this is a part of the course where the experienced men can pick up a fraction or two.

Subtle though the balance between the various forces is, there is no time actually to think about them. It is more an instinctive 'feel' than a conscious arrangement. When you get it right it feels right – but if you get it wrong you know instantly. Of course, this is racing, and you must have speed – the whole essence of racing being to keep, or even increase, speed where others might lose it – but a combination of speed and the wrong line will automatically take you off the course. In the old days they had straw bales at the Steilhang exit and several times I overshot slightly and collected some straw in my bindings that I couldn't remove until the finish. Nowadays there are safety nets which give about a metre more room for manoeuvre, but you still have to be very precise to come out of the Steilhang correctly.

Your exit brings you out onto a narrow wood path that requires a tuck position and a good, fast glide. This part of the course can be boring, but racers who let their concentration lapse do so at their own peril. When you are on the Steilhang you cannot actually see the exit road, but once you have reached it there is always a slight sense of relief. The steep and technical part of the course is behind you – the rest is tuck in and go. But letting that sense of relief overwhelm you can be disastrous. The wood path is always icy and rutted and the skis are rattling around as they try to work independently of each other; it is not an easy glide by any means and it pays to keep your wits about you all the time.

After this comes the Alte Schneise. This is a fast traverse, still heavily rutted, that is also taken in the tuck. Up until 1972 there were three rough bumps on this section that were really tough. One skier I saw fall here had broken his skis just below the tips, and his helmet was torn off by the force of the crash. If you fell you really took a purler, so the organisers levelled the course out with bull-dozers. It is still not easy traversing across a hill at speed, but those who do it correctly can pick up a lot of time.

From here to the Hausbergkante, the course is a series of long sweeping bends in the tuck that sap all your energy. The position is broken only momentarily on a couple of occasions, and the consequent strain on the thigh muscles is very great. But as your legs are becoming increasingly tired, so you have time to think about the Hausbergkante and the return to the steep for the drop to the finish.

If you are not in the first group, coming onto the Hausberg can be a problem with light. First-groupers have sunshine all the way, but later starters hit shade before they arrive at the actual jump, which can be very disconcerting.

It is important at this point not to spend too much time in the air. In ski racing time spent in the air is wasted time – it is always faster to have skis on the snow than flying through the air. The way to avoid air time is to make a little pre-jump just before the lip of the fall-away. This has the effect of avoiding the 'throw-off', ski-jump-like sensation, allowing you to go from flat to slope without cata-pulting far into the air.

Once this jump is negotiated, there is a sweeping left-hander across the hill with a small compression on entry before a tight tuck into the Zielschuss. About a hundred and fifty metres from the finish flags, however, there is a compression that can really take its toll on tired legs. From going down quite steeply, suddenly you are going up. At this stage your legs refuse to act quite as efficiently as shock absorbers as they did at the start, and the violent forces that the compression imposes have caught many a racer out within sight of the finish.

After the compression, it is just a short *schuss* – every nerve fighting for that last ounce of speed – to the finish gate.

In the finish area, after either a practice run or a race, there is always a sense of accomplishment. All the way down you feel that the mountain has been doing its best to trip you up. Half the time you are not racing against time or another competitor – you are just striving to stay on the course, man against mountain. Just getting to the finish area means you have beaten something, even if it isn't the other racers.

Kitzbühel may be my favourite for the adrenalin it produces, but there is nowhere like Wengen for character, atmosphere and sheer beauty. Just getting to the start is a pleasure. Wengen is a car-less town, so the transport to the top is rather special – a train. Instead of going up two-by-two on a chairlift, you are all in together, which is good for spirit and good for morale. It takes time of course, twenty-five minutes from Wengen to Kleine Scheidegg, but I would prefer to waste a few minutes on the train than take a chairlift any time.

At Scheidegg there is a short T-bar to the start-hut, where the view is nothing short of stunning. You are actually underneath the towering and brooding north face of the Eiger, looking across the box-like ravine of the Lauterbrunnen valley to Mürren and the Schilthorn on the other side. It is a view that I have never tired of – indeed, quite the opposite, the more I see it the more I marvel at it. Standing at the Wengen start-hut on a good day is a pure delight. The area is a sun-trap and the sun is warming, altogether a very friendly feeling. On a bad day, however, it can be a nightmare. Not only is there no view but the wind can cut bitterly over the Mann-lichen ridge. On days like that, when the Eiger and the Jungfrau hide their faces and the wind chills the bones, Wengen is not a pleasant place at all.

The Lauberhorn course itself starts off rather casually. There is time to settle down into a tuck and prepare for the first right-hand bend, though this has to be carved well. An open, wide section that runs over gentle rolls follows – but the trick is to keep accelerating by staying in a tight and compact downhill position with the skis as flat as possible on the snow. Speed really builds up here, reaching about 85mph, and you feel as if you are on top of the world. You feel you have time to enjoy yourself – there is no fear of straw bales or safety netting.

The red flags on the course slowly draw you to the left, lining you up for an incredibly tight 180-degree, hairpin corner. This slows you right down and you enter the Hundschopf at what seems a snail's pace. The line here is to head for the marker flag on the left which leads you through a narrow gap between a rising rocky cliff and some safety netting. Once you have hit this line and passed the flag, you don't so much jump as fall away. The Hundschopf is an imposing wall when seen for the first time – and it can still look pretty awesome even when you have seen it several times before – but it is not so adrenalin-producing when you actually ski it. One always has the impression, in spite of travelling at about 40mph, that one is going very slowly on the approach and there is a tendency to take the jump too casually.

No jump in downhilling should ever be treated in this way. On the Hundschopf, a jump too lightly taken can see the skier flying all the way to the bottom and hitting the flat with a bone-jarring thud. If nothing else, this will usually wake you up, but it also slows you right down. A bad jump here can lose time – but it is the next, crucial section of the course where the men are really sorted from the boys.

The Minschkante is a jump-cum-turn that requires quartz-precision timing. The approach is a fast, left-hand turn before the leap, but it is the landing where you have to be spot on. As your skis hit the snow, it is necessary simultaneously to initiate a long, sweeping right-hander that falls away. If you are not careful, you can be forced onto your uphill ski. If you fail to get this jump right, you will lose all your speed for the next part of the course, which requires good, controlled, fast gliding.

This section is a mountain road that sets you on a tightrope. If you are too aggressive you will edge too much, while if you are too light you will slide off the course. Again it is the 'feel' that comes from experience that will see you through this part of the Lauberhorn but about halfway along the road there is a very sharp right angle followed immediately by another. It is a bit like putting a chicane in the middle of the Mulsanne straight at Le Mans, and no amount of experience, or training, can prepare you for such an incredibly tricky and unique obstacle. You just have to claw your way around it as best you can.

This is a very narrow part of the course and it funnels you through a railway tunnel (the same tunnel that featured in the Robert Redford film *Downhill Racer*) before opening out again into an enervating, tight-tuck *schuss*. By this stage your legs are already beginning to feel the strain but you are only halfway: there is still a full minute to go.

The tuck position is broken for a short while for four contrived turns through marker gates, the last two of which are quite tight, but then you must fall quickly into it again for the fast Hanneggschuss – a steep and straight section that gets the speed back into the 80 to 90mph range within seconds. It is very exciting and very beautiful. Even though you are travelling faster than the legal limit on the road there seems to be time to enjoy the race and to look around a little. There is a lot of the course behind you and there are some difficult bits to come but here you can just tuck down and have fun.

A gentle (by racers' standards) 'S' leads you into the Austrian Hole. This is a drop-off which, on one occasion many years ago, caught out the whole of the Austrian team – hence its name. Apart from the drop-off there is a series of rollers and humps that really hurts the legs. With the tiredness that is now setting in fast the pressure of the wind tries to open you up, to break open your tuck position. Every ounce of strength is required to keep tight and low, for allowing yourself to open up would have the same effect as a parachute brake on an aeroplane. As you struggle to keep your speed up and to stay crouched, the track is getting narrower and narrower. The effect is to make you suddenly aware of your speed. No longer are you high-speed cruising: now you know you are racing. Although the body is nearing exhaustion, the sudden awareness of speed, and the realisation that the course now demands accuracy to within a few inches, is stimulating. More adrenalin is produced here than at any other part of the course. There is a machine-gun rattle as your skis clatter over the ice, and it is a struggle to get any grip. The ice is like boiler plate, and just getting an edge is a problem. Every cell in the body has to be alert – there isn't room for even the tiniest mistake.

Many races have been won or lost on this section: the skill with which the last 'S' turn is skied has decided many a Lauberhorn. Peter Müller lost it at the final jump after these turns in 1982 and Andy Mill finished his career here. It's only a matter of feet from the finish, but it has broken many a dream.

After the race, in the finish area of the longest downhill on the circuit, there is a real feeling of pleasure. In Kitzbühel it is man against mountain, in Wengen it is man and mountain together. To ski both is to experience all the variety that the mountains can offer.

Both Kitzbühel and Wengen are classic courses. They are courses with traditions and histories and they ask you to ski the mountain. If you ski on a road it is because there is a road there under the snow waiting to be used in the summer. The mountain itself and the way man has used it determines the course.

This is not so in Yugoslavia. The man-made course that has been set up at Sarajevo for the 1984 Olympics is a hotch-potch of contrived obstacles. There is nothing real about it. It is a bit like phoney 'antique' furniture, it does the job but there is always something shoddy about it. There is certainly no sense of man and mountain in battle. It is very hard to find any enthusiasm for it.

To start with, there wasn't even a mountain. They had to build a three-storey restaurant at the top of the hill to comply with the vertical height difference that FIS required for the registration of a downhill course.

The advantage, of course, is that this makes for the most convenient start-hut on the circuit. A chairlift takes you into the restaurant building and you then walk up one flight of stairs to the dining room and another flight to the start-hut. This is connected to the mountain proper by a ramp packed with snow that is the first part of the course, which means that other racers can actually sit in the restaurant and watch the early starters literally shoot past the window! But although the start is fun, it is the only part of the course that meets any of the criteria for a good downhill track.

The first problem is that, once out of the start, you have to make a left-hand turn before any speed has been built up. This leads into a right-hander with a wider exit, and it is only at this stage that downhill racing speeds are being achieved. For the next several hundred metres you can enjoy the only satisfying part of the course. A fairly long, straight approach leads to a very pleasant jump. It doesn't shake or jolt – it is one of those jumps where one second you are skiing, the next you are weightless. The landing is steep so there is no crunch, just a smooth jump onto a fast landing.

At the bottom of the jump you are carrying quite a steady speed but the course carries you right onto a ridge that is marked by prevailing winds from the left. When I was there in 1983 the winds didn't bother us too much, but I am assured we were lucky and that quite strong gusting is the rule rather than the exception. If those conditions are struck during the Olympic race it will make a mockery of the form book as just one good gust can set a racer back a full second.

From the ridge, a left- and right-hander in quick succession follow the natural terrain of the mountain – but this is the last bit of natural skiing on the course. Although you are coming into the tree-line in a tuck for what should be a very fast *schuss*, the organisers have decided, quite inexplicably in my view, to put what amounts to a giant slalom section into the track. Apparently this was done in an attempt to slow the racer down, but it shows little imagination. No downhiller likes contrived turns through flags. From the time it was first conceived, our sport has involved getting from top to bottom of a mountain in the quickest way possible. It is all right, or at least it can be all right, to build an obstacle into a course with a bulldozer. A few mounds or a tight turn will slow the skier down with what appear to be quite natural hazards – but just to put flags on a down-hill course and ask racers to ski through them as though they were Stenmark or Phil Mahre doing a giant slalom is ridiculous; to me it takes away the whole meaning of downhill racing.

But these flag turns aren't the only contrived parts of the course. All the way down from this point the course is an avenue through the trees; but it isn't a natural break in the forest, it was done with chainsaws. The avenue is exactly the same width from the start of the tree-line to the finish. It is so artificial that you know it is man trying to catch you out here – the mountain has nothing to do with it at all.

Sometime during the planning stages of this course someone must have said: 'Let's put in some jumps to break the monotony.' Heads undoubtedly nodded in agreement as bulldozers were dispatched to build two consecutive ridges across the course: they are disasters. Although taken at speed, there is no fall-away on the landing and the second comes immediately after the first. The effect is jump . . . plop, jump . . . plop – a little like the sensation of walking in diving flippers, except that these landings hurt more. Because you are hitting the ground hard, and with speed, the shocks travel right up through the body and aching limbs have to discover new limits of endurance. Unfortunately the bulldozer man must have got carried away because there are about ten more, equally lacklustre, leaps to come.

After the first two, however, there is a straight section to get the speed back up before a sweeping right-hander. This turn needs to be delayed as long as possible so that it can be started close to the safety fence. The reason is that a roller has been built into the exit of the turn, and if you don't delay long enough the wrong line into the roller will stop you keeping enough height for the next part of the course. This is a characterless right-angled left-hander, the exit being another jump with a flat, jarring landing. But, while your muscles are still screaming in protest, you have to be aware enough to delay into a double-gated right-hander: for it is necessary to go wide into the first gate so that you can be tight into the second on the exit. Only this way can you get direction for another teeth-knocking, back-jarring, knee-hurting, toe-ramming jump onto the flat.

From here on the course is straight to the finish – but there are still forty-five seconds to go! This is no fast *schuss* for the gliding experts; rather, it is like falling down a staircase. All the way down there are contrived leaps but you can't just put your head down and go. These jumps contain hidden horrors. In 1983 Peter Müller got a little off-line at one, caught an edge, and landed with his body on the take-off point of the next. It was such a bad fall that he had to be airlifted out.

About ten seconds from the finish there is a veritable Cape Canaveral launching pad. At race speeds this can be a sixty-metre leap – and this even when you are trying to stay on the snow – but fortunately the landing isn't too flat, otherwise the racers would get to the finish area with their kneecaps under their armpits.

Once in the finish area, your only satisfaction is that you have done your day's work. You're also glad to have got down in one piece. Franz Klammer said after the 1983 race, in which he came third, that he would have gone faster had he felt safe. That comment is a real indictment of the course.

When ski racing carries such huge sponsorship and television audiences it seems absurd that FIS cannot come up with a better course. When we first saw it, many of us said to the FIS delegate that the jumps were going to be a real problem. His reaction was: 'Ski it anyway and we'll see later.' He wouldn't take the word of the racers, saying, in effect, ski it and if there are any accidents we will think again. That sort of attitude is intolerable in modern day downhilling, when racers are already very close to the limit.

After the 1983 races the organisers realised that they would have to make some changes before the Olympics, but there will be some real problems. At the moment the course depends on snow conditions to an unusual extent. If there is little snow all the jumps are horrendous, but if there is a heavy snow dump many of the hollows between the jumps would be filled in and the course would ski completely differently. (In fact a relatively small amount of snow affects an 'artificial' course much more than a 'natural' one.) What it boils down to is that the track was badly designed in the first place, and in an ideal world it would be scrapped completely and the designers sent back to their drawing boards.

Apart from the practical elements of course design, the Sarajevo track is almost faceless. Because it is new and man-made, the turns and jumps have no names – it is just turn one, turn two and jump one, jump two and so on, which adds to the general lack of character. Even if the course becomes established and the turns and jumps do acquire names with the passing years, it will never be a Kitzbühel or a Wengen. It will never be a 'classic' downhill.

—11—
THE
FINAL YEAR

The day after my second at Val Gardena I woke up in my bedroom and looked up at the cup sitting on the bedside table. The day before seemed like a dream and I hit myself on the head to make sure I wasn't still sleeping.

Not only was I not dreaming, but things generally were running true to form. After we had packed up the team van to leave the resort, the key was turned in the ignition and the damn thing wouldn't start. The only way we could leave Val Gardena was by getting a push-start from one of the race officials. That put my feet very firmly back on the ground!

Next stop was Crans Montana and what, for me, was a very difficult race. My good result had put me into the spotlight and the whole of the ski world was looking to see if it was just a flash in the pan. That put me under great pressure, from myself as well as the press, to prove that I was really worthy of my first-fifteen place.

When we arrived at the hotel in Crans I was met by a thick wad of congratulatory telegrams. Naturally I was very pleased but, at the same time, surprised that there seemed to be more from my friends in motor racing than from people in skiing. I didn't dwell on this, however, and was happy just to get to a telephone to call Willy Bailey, who was working in Geneva. We had a long, emotional conversation and Willy was actually crying in his happiness for me. In some ways he was the only one alive who really knew what it all meant. He had been there in the days of hand-to-mouth living, and he knew how much effort and privation had gone into the ten-year battle for such a result. It was wonderful talking to him. My only regret was that Peter Fuchs was not there as well. To have been able to have a few bottles with Peter would have made everything perfect.

On the first Crans practice day I was free skiing with Todd Brooker and Robin McLeish in beautiful powder snow. Having just been second in the world, I felt really exuberant; merely having skis on my feet felt exciting. I played games in the powder with the others and enjoyed free skiing more than I had for many a long day. Even a purler I took off a twenty-foot cliff into the deep snow was enjoyable!

I had never particularly liked the Crans Montana course, but when I left the starting gate at the beginning of the race I was aware, really for the very first time, that winning was on the cards. In fact I was fifteenth in the race – only two-hundredths from sixteenth, but this time on the right side of the line and with another World Cup point. The result was much more important than that, however. It meant that I would be in the top fifteen when the new list was drawn up, and therefore in the first group for the World Championships at Schladming.

My earlier success at Val Gardena produced another, unexpected benefit – an offer from Mercedes of the use of a car for the rest of the season. It meant that I could be independent of the team bus and get to race sites quicker and more comfortably. That Merc estate was a godsend: for Schladming it was worth its weight in gold, as it meant that, in spite of a nine-hour trip from Crans, I arrived in good shape to ski the following day. A trip that long in the bus would have left me feeling pretty shaken for a day or so – enough, in fact, to limit the effectiveness of the first day of practice. As it was I was fresh for practice, my first with the top group.

For the first training run I was drawn number eight with Leonard Stock in front of me and Franz Klammer behind. Being in the first fifteen meant much more than mere satisfaction at having made it: it meant that I was skiing on a course with virtually no tracks. I didn't have to worry about being caught out by the ruts of the early runners – I was one myself now, and I found the experience to my liking.

For the first time in my life everything began to go as I had always hoped that it would. My skis were running, and I was skiing well up to my top-group position in practice. Even more than that, I was skiing the first two-thirds of the course as fast, if not faster, than anyone else. The Austrians were taking notice of me – I was considered one of the main threats to their skiers – and I seemed to be getting faster and faster as training progressed.

There were only two problems. The first was that the organisers had introduced a combined event into the programme. This was a separate downhill and slalom, the downhill to be run two days before the actual championship downhill. I had to compete in it to get the FIS points needed to safeguard my first group position. I didn't agree with the race, and I said so at every opportunity, but I had to take part in order to keep in touch with the top. To get the points the requirement was that a racer completed both stages of the race – downhill and slalom. At the start of the slalom Stuart Fitzsimmons, who was there as the team video man, held a placard out in front of me. It said: 'Don't laugh.' It was appropriate, as I didn't ski the course with any intention of attacking. Instead I skied it like a ski instructor – fifteen seconds behind everyone else. This, of course, was to ensure that I finished and got my points: it was a ridiculous thing to have to do. The Austrian race commentators were amused at Stuart's sign, the more staid British management were less so. It attracted the attention of Phil Mahre, too, who said to Stuart after the 'race': 'It's good that someone has seen this race for what it is.'

The other problem was the weather.

In the calendar for the Championships the programme had been for the combined downhill to be on the Thursday, the championship downhill on the Saturday and the combined slalom the following Tuesday. The weather was so bad, though, that the organisers tried moving the combined downhill back to the Friday, meaning that we would have had to race a downhill on two consecutive days.

As it turned out, even this wasn't possible, and the organisers had to put off both downhills until the following week. The revised programme required us to ski the slalom first on Tuesday, with the downhills on Friday and Saturday, following a Thursday practice day. This was a major disaster. Programmes are not just orders of events, they are timetables for training and race build-up. The preparation schedule was now shattered: the slalom which we had expected to ski last was first, and we had to ski two downhills one after the other.

In the Thursday downhill practice I skied the course quite well and felt I had something in reserve over the last third or so; but when I looked at the times I found I was fifth fastest. I was really surprised. I knew that I could go a bit faster and I knew that if I did I could easily find myself on the podium again.

But first came the combined downhill on the Friday. I disappointed myself by coming only seventh. I didn't ski badly, but I couldn't understand why I was a second slower than the winner, Conradin Cathomen. Koni Rupprechter and I watched the videos over and over but could not come up with anything wrong. It was a mystery. Perhaps one of the reasons was that I didn't want to ski the race. I had to ski it for the points, but my real target was the championship race on Saturday – it could have been that just not wanting to ski had enough effect on my attitude to slow me down that vital second.

I went out on the Saturday determined to put matters right, and things started off incredibly well. Over the first four seconds of the course I was actually the fastest – one-tenth faster than Harti Weirather – but by the first main split-time at halfway I had dropped three-tenths. This still put me very much in touch but the temperature, and therefore the snow condition, was four degrees up on the Thursday training which was having an effect on my time.

At the second split, two-thirds of the way down, I was in ninth place and doing quite well when disaster struck. I took a fast left-hander a fraction too early and came out too low, only just managing, literally by the proverbial coat of varnish, to avoid the safety net. This meant that I had to throw my skis around for the turn out, and the manoeuvre cost precious time.

I picked up again on the last part of the course and had the seventh fastest speed over that section, but when I looked at the clock in the finish area I knew that my time was not good enough. That one mistake had blown it.

I felt I had let everyone down. In the training I had known we were in with a real chance, and now I had made a silly mistake and let a good result slip through my fingers. I was bitterly disappointed and annoyed. I had set a standard at Val Gardena and had really felt that I could maintain it; now I had to live with throwing it away. Although it was frustrating I had to adopt Steve Podborski's attitude of forgetting the race just gone and concentrating on the next one: the old don't-cry-over-spilt-milk, buy-a-new-bottle theory.

Before the season started I had intended to retire after these championships, but after Val Gardena I had been in two minds. Some of my friends were encouraging me to go on, while others were telling me to quit while I was ahead. I decided to leave it until after the last race at Aspen before making my final decision.

The racing for the rest of the season went quite well. I was a close thirteenth at Garmisch and other results, although not quite as good, told me that I wasn't drifting too far away.

At Aspen there were two races. I had a poor race in the first but in the second things went much better. I wasn't too quick at the top of the course, but picked up on the later sections, and I remember thinking to myself as I was skiing it: 'Gosh, if I can ski like this over the technical sections I just have to go on.' I was fifteenth in that race – another World Cup point, making twenty-five for the season – and I would start in the first group from the beginning of the 1982–83 season. I had always dreamed of that sort of position so there wasn't really a chance of me giving up. That final Aspen race had convinced me that I had to continue to try for even more improvement. I determined not to think of retirement again for another twelve months.

That summer I put everything into my preparation. A friend had opened a fitness centre called Bodys in the Kings Road in London, and another friend, bob-sledder and former decathlete Nick Phipps, was on the coaching staff. It was a perfect opportunity for me to work on my own body.

Nick, being a winter sports man himself, knew something of the physical requirements of downhilling and he had experience of tuning the body to optimum condition. Together we worked to get me stronger, faster and fitter than ever before. The work was mainly at the centre (I had decided not to ski too much in the summer so as to be fresh and hungry when I finally got to the snow) and, with Nick training with me, things really started to come together.

But if I was to do as well as I hoped I knew I would need good back-up on the team. One of the problems with small teams is that you don't have the same flow of information as the big ones, and I knew that it was ridiculous to kid myself that results would come if I didn't have the right sort of back-up. This would mean a coach and a deputy, a video man and a masseur. We would also need the equipment – radio and video hardware – and committed co-operation from the servicemen of the ski companies.

In the early days the British Federation had always denied such resources, saying that we were not getting the results to warrant them. Now we had the results, the team was being run by a paid Alpine Director, and yet it was apparent that I was worse off than ever before. There was no coach and Dave Richmond, the amazingly hard-working team assistant, had had a letter saying that if he wanted to go on he had to do it for nothing. On top of this the proposed budget for the year was lower than any year I could remember.

I knew the Federation of old, so I knew that if I wanted results, I would have to organise things myself behind the scenes. Bang went any chance of a holiday.

The first thing was to get some money. Koni Rupprechter had been offered a contract featuring a big cut in salary, which he naturally saw no reason to accept. Just to have a coach I had to get some money to boost the salary offer, as well as money to pay Dave Richmond and video man Stuart Fitzsimmons. This meant dividing my time between the weight room and the telephone.

Meanwhile other things were happening to frustrate me further. A week before I thought I would be going off to Greece for the first event under my Rothmans rally programme, I was told that there was no car available. I was really, really disappointed. I had had my appetite whetted for this sport and I enjoyed its professional atmosphere. All that summer I had done nothing but train and hustle for ski team money. I had been looking forward to getting away from it all for a while in Greece with some serious rallying. For weeks I had thought about little else. Now that aspiration was nipped in the bud and all I had to look forward to was more fitness work and more hustling.

One bright spot was an invitation to join in the *Superstars* programme on television. This gave me another incentive to train and I really knuckled under with Nick, who knew something of the game as he had helped train Brian Hooper for his *Superstars* success.

For me, the *Superstar* heat itself was interesting but not much fun. The other competitors took things very seriously, with managers and trainers permanently in tow, and I was not up to the mark in running to be competitive with them. I enjoyed the cycling and did quite well and, in the gym tests, I missed out on setting a new record by only two jumps. This was a disappointment because there was a prize of a colour telly for new records and I had set myself that telly as a target. Still, I did come third of eight starters. *Superstars* gave new impetus to my training programme and I was glad to have had a break from the daily grind.

On the sponsorship side, Remy Martin came up trumps. They agreed to a deal, after some protracted negotiations, that gave us enough cash to pay Koni and just about enough to pay Stuart and Dave. Naturally they wanted some return on their investment and we wore black and gold suits, the Remy colours, for the rest of that season: about as much as the amateur rules would allow.

So by the end of September I finally had a coach, and off we went for the customary hibernation at Hintertux for the first work of the new season on snow. On the way there I flew from Zurich to Innsbruck by Tyrolean Airways, and the pilot took us on a little mountain-hopping – we took the scenic route.

It was wonderful being in the mountains again. The successes of the previous season flooded back into my mind and I was really psyched up by the time we landed at Innsbruck. I felt this could really be my year. I was certainly fitter than I had ever been and the last race at Aspen had rekindled my belief in my own skiing ability. Everything seemed to be on my side and I was keen to start.

In the training, I was skiing technically better than I had ever skied before. With Koni and Stuart I had the nucleus of a team that worked well and Martin Bell, along with his younger brother who was training with the team, was showing real potential.

The Federation's Alpine Director, Fraser Clyde, had been successful in getting us a physio and Diane Ouzman joined us in November. For the first time we had a full crew. Time trials with the Canadians showed we were in with a chance. We were competitive with them and morale was high – all we needed was the snow.

But no snow came.

The first downhill of the season had been set for Laax in Switzerland, but by race day no snow had arrived and the event was transferred to Pontresina. I was disappointed by the enforced change in schedule, as I knew the Laax course but had never skied the Pontresina course on Lagalb before. When I did see it for the first time my disappointment was reinforced. It turned out to be a very twisty and turny course – not really suited to my style of skiing – with rock showing through the piste.

Many of the racers were damaging their skis on the rocks, so I used only my very oldest pair in training. Even so I was happy enough with the way things were going. We were reasonably close even on the old skis, and I thought that once we had the race skis out, we would be in business.

For the race I drew start number two – an Englishman was to be second down the hill for the first race of the season! – which was a good number for the conditions. I was very eager and confident when I launched myself onto the course.

Everything went well and I had no complaints with the run – there were a couple of turns that I wasn't one hundred per cent satisfied with but that is about par for the course anyway – but I slipped in the final result to twenty-seventh place. The time was only half a second down on the top fifteen, but it was disappointing to have to start the season with a detailed analysis of what went wrong.

On my serviceman's hand-timing at the top I was one of the quickest, but by the intermediate time I had dropped a second and a half. Somewhere in that middle thirty seconds something had gone drastically wrong. In the tight turns at the bottom of the course I was tenth quickest – faster even than Klammer who finished second – so whatever it was that had gone wrong was only to do with the long traverse in the middle of the race.

The next race, at Val d'Isère, was totally different. For the first time in the season we had fresh snow to ski on and in the resort itself we found ourselves in the friendly atmosphere of the Hotel Le Clos of the Club Mark Warner.

My friend, Bob Miller, had flown over from Canada to assist (I had asked him to do this as he had a very good eye for the finer points of ski racing, and I needed his expertise badly) and a new Audi Quattro, courtesy of Audi Sport UK, had been driven out for my use by Mike Jardine of Europa Sport.

To top it all we had smiles on our faces because Willy Bailey was in town. He had come over from Verbier to visit me, and it was just like old times. The whole team was in good spirits and we were among friends. The training was going really well and Willy, who could drag a smile from even the most acerbic person, was on top form. His presence was extra-specially welcome as bad weather set in and the race was eventually cancelled. While this lasted we had a lot of time on our hands, and it was important to keep our morale high. With Willy Bailey in the camp that was never a problem.

Although there was no race in Val d'Isère I felt there was no need for concern. Everything we had done on the mountain had gone well and the skis seemed to be running. When the organisers made their decision to call it off so that we could travel to Val Gardena I was feeling as though everything was on course for another good result. Certainly I had no reason to think otherwise. Val Gardena had been good to me before and I was confident I could make it good for me again.

The course that year was bumpier than it had ever been before, but it was still good to ski. A lot of entertainment was provided on the video in the evening watching people fall, but my own first day of practice went satisfyingly well. I was a little unsettled by a poor final practice but I didn't lose heart and I knew that I could get things right on the day.

However, bad weather set in again on the Saturday and the race was put off until Sunday – another day to wait.

On the Sunday morning I looked out of my window to see a really beautiful day. The mountain was looking glorious and I was looking forward to the race. On the cable car up I decided that, as the visibility was good, I would get away from everyone and warm up with a run to the bottom of free skiing. I didn't go overboard on this, letting my body warm up gently, and I sensibly slowed down for a couple of bumps that I could see looming up ahead. But even though I was taking it quite easily, I caught an edge and twisted over my downhill ski. I flipped over a couple of times, nothing too serious, finally ending up in the soft snow beside the piste.

I couldn't move. Any attempt to do so resulted in shooting pains from the centre of my back, and I knew I had landed on something hard under the snow.

Eventually Martin Bell skied down to me. He helped me to my feet and I managed to side-slip slowly down the hill. Racers were shooting past me on their warm-ups, and I thought to myself that the injury was going to make things difficult when I joined them in the race proper. Pain was stabbing down from my back into my right leg, but I didn't give a thought to not taking part in the race.

At the bottom I bumped into Dave Richmond coming out of the

167

ski room, so I threw him my skis and told him to get Di (the team physio) and a doctor quickly. In my room, just getting my clothes off was agony, but I managed it by taking things gently. By the time I had finished Koni, Di and the doctor arrived. I was lying on my back on the bed and when the doctor asked me to roll over, I couldn't. The pain was so bad – excruciating – that I couldn't move at all. The doctor and Di between them had to roll me over.

After his examination the doctor was sure there was no structural damage to my back; he decided that the problem was severe bruising to the spine. He prescribed pain-killers, and I knew then that there was to be no race for me at Val Gardena that year. Even if I made a miraculous recovery overnight I would not have sufficient co-ordination after the pain-killers to ski the second race. The bottom had fallen out of my world.

When they had all gone and I was lying alone in my room, misery flooded in on me. I wasn't getting any younger, I needed results to be able to justify continuing on the circuit, but I could hardly get those results if I was lying in bed. There was no pot of gold at the end of my career, and I knew that I really had to start thinking about the future. The blackest thoughts crowded in on me, made worse by the thought that the other racers were out on the hill skiing for *my* race. Of all the races of the season, this was the one (two, as it turned out, because of the Val d'Isère cancellation) that I was most keyed up for. To have to give it up because of a silly, free-skiing fall was the cruellest possible blow; in my depression I could see little to look forward to in the future.

But soon the pain-killing drugs put paid to all these black thoughts – they made me as high as a kite, and I was able to struggle downstairs to watch the race on television. The pain in my back was nothing to the pain of watching Erwin Resch standing on the second place podium behind Conradin Cathomen. The memory of standing on the podium myself was still fresh in my mind; having Resch occupy it now was really rubbing salt in, as it was Resch who had just pipped me the year before.

On the Monday I watched the next race – this time to see Franz Klammer ski to a win – and left Val Gardena the following day to fly to London for a thorough medical examination and an X-ray. Fortunately these revealed that the local doctor had been correct, and I was told that the only cure was rest. I had time for this as it was now the Christmas break on the circuit, so I flew out again with my girlfriend to spend Christmas with my parents in Austria.

I was usually able to enjoy these breaks with my family and relax but, this time, Lady Luck was coming down unfairly hard on me. Either I ate something bad or I caught a stomach bug, but whatever it was I spent that Christmas as sick as a dog. I could not eat my Christmas dinner and life seemed black once more. The attack left me weak and my back was still hurting, but eventually I was able gingerly to attempt a few runs on skis. At first every turn and tuck was really painful, but it got less and less so with every run and before long I felt ready to race again.

The first downhill of 1983 was at Morzine, where we were welcomed by what seemed like the same rain we had left behind in 1982. Despite the weather all the racers were going through the motions of preparing for a race and I, too, drove up to the finish area to look at the course. It was the picture of desolation. There was hardly any snow right up to the tree-line. I realised that the chances of a race being held were at least five hundred to one against. Koni agreed with me and, even though the organisers had still not formally abandoned the race, we decided to go to Val d'Isère for the British Championships. I needed race practice after my accident and at least I would be able to get that in Val. So, after spending only eighteen hours in Morzine we were on the road again.

Before leaving we rang Fraser Clyde in Val d'Isère to let him know we were coming and arrived at the hotel about seven in the evening. Fraser met us and I said I would like to go over my expenses with him. He said he was too busy just then but would be happy to do it later. That was the last I saw of him.

In training the next day my back was much more painful than I had expected, and I was able to do only one of the runs; but just that one was enough to tell me that the course was not suitable for a British Championship downhill. It was the same course as the World Cup but it was even faster than it had been in 1982. Martin Bell underestimated the compression and crashed quite badly, injuring his elbow, so I travelled up to the top to warn his brother, Graham. Despite the warning Graham crashed at exactly the same place and hurt his ankle.

In two runs the British team was virtually decimated, a ridiculous state of affairs. It is true that the British Championship race qualified for FIS points, but to ask young British racers with limited experience to ski on a course this tough was insanity. There was more to come.

Once the Morzine race was cancelled the World Cup committee decided to hold an alternative race at Val d'Isère. This sounded fine: I should have been able to ski my own championships, and then ski the course all over again for the World Cup. But it wasn't to be. The committee, in their wisdom, decided that if I skied the British Championships I would be barred from competing in the World Cup race. The argument went something like this: I had been entered for the Morzine race and now wanted to ski the British race; if I did I would be excluded from the World Cup; but anyone who skied in the British Championships who wasn't entered for the Morzine race could legally ski the World Cup race. The reasoning was that we were not to be allowed to race in two races set for the same time – but it was a stupid interpretation of the rules. All the organisers were trying to do was stop us getting more practice than other racers (although anyone who raced who hadn't been to Morzine would have got this anyway) and the effect was to prohibit me from skiing in my own country's championship. The fact that I wouldn't have been able to race because of my back was irrelevant. It was another example of officials forgetting what sport was about.

In training for the World Cup race I felt like the hunchback of Notre Dame. Only lengthy physiotherapy sessions with Di were able to get me through it. I could not test the skis properly because I was unable to get into a tight tuck, and at the end of each day my back was so sore I could hardly stand up. But I knew I had to race. To miss out on these two races would have meant a loss of four in all – nearly half a season – and I could not allow that. As well as Di I tried the Canadian physio, Terry Spence, alias 'Too Loose': anything to get my back better.

The night before the race Fraser Clyde came into the dining-room very briefly and whispered something to Koni. My ears picked up something about Di Ouzman and the girls' team, but I couldn't hear very well. When Fraser was gone, I asked Koni what it was all about. He told me it was nothing and not to worry about it.

In the morning I spoke to Di about the pre-race massage. I had to have a half-hour session to loosen up the muscles around my spine just to be able to finish, and I wanted to make sure we would both be in the same place at the same time so that we could get it done. But Di told me she didn't know if she would be there as Fraser had told her she had to go off with the girls' team as the physio.

I couldn't believe it. We were a team and working well, and now, when I needed a physio more than at any time in my career, she was to be taken away from me. This threw me into a real rage. No one seemed concerned with the cause of getting good British results. Clyde was the Alpine Director of the teams and he was being paid for the job: I had been largely responsible for securing the Peter Stuyvesant sponsorship that paid him, and now he was taking away my physio. He might just as well have been taking away my skis. I may have been injured but I knew, and Fraser Clyde knew, that I was capable of good results if I got the professional physiotherapy Di could give. To have her sent away at this time, with a girls' team that consistently occupied the last places in their races, was incomprehensible to me. It was absurd, and I wasn't going to accept it.

I told Koni that if they took Di away, that was it – there was no point in my going on. He intervened, and thankfully Di was there at the start, but psychologically the damage had been done. Fraser had scuttled my build-up for the race just as surely as if he had stolen my boots. There was not much spirit inside me when I jumped out of the starting gate for the first race.

Once on the course, though, all my troubles left me. The track was in fantastic condition, the sun was shining, I was carving good turns and I felt I was skiing really well. It was bliss. The wind in my face blew away the earlier dejection, and that run brought back to me the great joys that ski racing can give.

I made a tiny mistake in the compression, but it was not much, and at the bottom I was very pleased with my run. I was pleased, too, that Di's treatment had worked. I was able to stand up without too much pain and I was certain that I had done myself credit.

But I was too slow. I had skied well but the skis had not done the job. I knew I would have to try different ones the next day.

The following morning at breakfast Fraser Clyde came in and

wished me good luck. I ignored him. It was the first time he had spoken to me since the night we arrived and he wasn't my favourite person. He repeated his morning greeting a little louder. Without looking up, I let fly with some four-letter words. I just didn't need him around, especially just before a race. I was annoyed that the man was getting paid for doing nothing better than intrigue against me. Di worked herself flat out for no pay at all and Dave Richmond often put in sixteen-hour days for a total of £1500 a year. Both had their services taken for granted by Fraser. If he had left that room in a flash it couldn't have been quick enough for me.

The general atmosphere in Val d'Isère was as nasty as any I could remember. For the first time in years of skiing my car had the aerial broken off, the windscreen was spat on and obscenities, in English, were scrawled on the side. At the start of the second race only a motor racing friend, Derek Bell, could find the time to come up and wish me luck. Derek said he was glad to see that somebody other than him was nervous at the start; and I was nervous, make no mistake. His friendly greeting was much appreciated but there were no such greetings from Federation officials, despite the fact that there were half-a-dozen top Federation people in the resort.

If I hadn't had Shauna, my girlfriend, with me, all this would have got to me even more than it did. The pettiness of Fraser and the Federation, coupled with the pain in my back, could easily have broken my spirit if Shauna hadn't been there to back me up. She was aghast at the treatment I was getting and just having her there was enough to give me sufficient armour to ward off the barbs and the insults. Even so, once the second race was over, I was glad to get out of Val d'Isère.

The next race was Wengen. There the wonder of the landscape and the brilliance of the weather put me in an altogether different mood. I was in a hotel that I liked and I was sharing it with the Americans and Canadians who were my friends. The atmosphere was as different from Val d'Isère as it possibly could be.

In training things went like a dream. The skis were suddenly running and I was about fifth quickest on the top flats. Overall I was twelfth in both official practices and I was skiing easily up to my first fifteen standing. I was ready to get in amongst the points again.

But I figured without the weather. On Friday morning it started to snow and from having just enough snow for the race we suddenly had too much: it snowed all day Friday and well into Saturday. By race time there was still too much cloud and wind at the start and, after an initial delay, the race was postponed until the following day. But when I woke up on Sunday morning it was snowing heavily again. It was the last straw. I was really in with a chance and my dream was shattered again; even the weather seemed to be against me.

The result was that there were to be two races at Kitzbühel: the third double-up of the season. The pressure weighed heavily on me. I had to do well but I had never been closer than twenty-second on the Hahnenkamm and I knew that I would have to pull out all the stops if I was to produce a result that would salvage my self-respect.

But what an embarrassing week. In the first training run I went out to bomb the course, and I was six seconds behind. Even though I had never been a Kitzbühel specialist I knew that I hadn't skied the course that badly; there was worse to come. In the first of the two races I had a split-time equal to Uli Spiess, who finished sixth, but I could manage only forty-first at the bottom. The only minor satisfaction was that I finished eight places better than Franz Klammer, in the year that he went on to take the overall World Cup downhill title!

In the second race I crashed. I thought I had already crashed everywhere possible on the Hahnenkamm but somehow managed to find a new place, on the Hausbergkante. It was another bitter disappointment, but there were four races to go and I still had a chance to come back.

At Sarajevo, though, it was the same old story. After the first practice run I went through the back pages of the results but couldn't find my name so I went to the front, to find that I was fifth quickest. Once again I was back in the running in training only to have my hopes dashed with a miserable race result. For the second practice I started with number one, but as soon as I saw my time I knew it was hopeless. Steve Podborski came down after me, two seconds quicker, while the racer who followed him was two seconds faster again. I wasn't even in the running.

I still didn't doubt my own ability – I had after all been fifth the day before – but race-day disappointment was becoming too much of a habit. All I could do was hope that my luck would change for this race: but it didn't. I was thinking too much on the course – all the instinctive responses were gone and my timing was way off. I knew I was trying too hard, but I didn't know how to find the happy medium between that and not trying hard enough.

Earlier in the year John Samuel had suggested that perhaps I was too much concerned with organisation, sponsors and the like, to be able to give my full attention to skiing. I had to agree with him – but I didn't have any other choice. I needed proper organisation if I was to be able to ski at all and I couldn't have that unless I arranged it myself. After all, there is a lot more to skiing than just stepping into a pair of skis and skiing off: I knew that I had to have proper back-up and that no one else was going to arrange it for me – not to the level at which it became effective, anyway. I also knew there would come a time when the skiing had to stop. I had no trade or profession to fall back on and I had to take responsibility for my own future. By involving myself in the business and sponsorship side of skiing I was trying to create possibilities for the day when I would have to hang up my boots.

John was probably right. I might have been a better skier and had better results if I had been able to ski as worry-free as the Swiss and Austrians did but, being a British skier, I had to face facts. If I hadn't concerned myself with the backroom side of things I probably wouldn't have been able to ski at all: and skiing with a disadvantage was a hell of a lot better than that.

Of course I was skiing with an even greater disadvantage now. There were only three races left and I had no FIS points. For hour after hour I would watch the videos comparing this year's races with last year's, one racer against another, in an attempt to find an answer. It was a boring and lonely vigil and I couldn't have done my eyes any good staring at that tiny screen in stony and melancholy silence.

The worst moment of frustration was watching Peter Luescher exiting the 'esses' after the compression at Val d'Isère. Peter nearly blew it. He had to throw his skis sideways in order to make the turn and slowed himself down considerably. But overall he was faster than me, and I had skied that corner well. Whatever the reason – and I never really found out what it was – I couldn't accept it. Peter skied badly and made a mistake, I skied well, and yet he beat me. Watching that all but killed my spirit; I didn't know what to do.

St Anton, the next race, was head down and do it or bust. But my head was down too far, and I was skiing virtually blind. I hit a bump, and got thrown way off line before a flat section. That was the end of that. I needed a miracle now.

There were three weeks to go before the last two races of the year in America, so I had something of a breather. Koni took some of my skis off to get them specially ground. He had some contacts in the business and made himself responsible for preparing the skis for America. Atomic, too, promised me a pair specially prepared for American conditions, so I was going to have something to compare Koni's skis against.

In the meantime I went off to Val d'Isère to free-ski, to try to rediscover some enjoyment in the sport. Bad luck and bad results had taken their toll and I was skiing as a job – I knew I had to start loving it again to be able to come back. Fortunately, I found some friends in Val and together we had a good time. I started to get things back in perspective. I had arrived in the resort with a long face, but after a while my friends told me to snap out of it. With their help I began to realise that what had happened wasn't the end of the world. Even though I had been on the circuit all my adult life (and a good part of my childhood!), it was still a case of 'if at first you don't succeed . . .'.

The only trouble was that, although I was able to sort out my own mind, I found sorting out the Federation more difficult. The impossible I could do, miracles took a little longer. The problem was that I was not sure whether I was going to be able to go to America. Even though I was committed to the whole of the World Cup season, and the American races were to be my last chance, the Federation dithered about whether or not to let me go. By this stage I was well used to their ways, so was not overly surprised. I worked on them, of course, as did Koni, and eventually, ten days before departure, it was decided I could go. The budget was very tight, but at least I had the green light.

For the first training run at Aspen I used Koni's skis and when I got to the end of the top flats I had a smile on my face. These skis were accelerating. By the time I got to the steep pitch called Aztec I was actually laughing. I made a hash of the turns and I wasn't skiing with the rhythm that I would have liked, but my time was promising. For the second run I used the Atomic skis. The difference was startling. Again I felt the deadness and dullness that I had felt all winter. The time on the flats was slower; with Koni's skis I had been fifth fastest on this section but with the Atomic 'Specials' I couldn't even make the top twenty-five.

I tried out some other skis which were so-so, but on the last practice day I used another pair of the skis Koni had prepared and I was second fastest at the top. Even though I made a real mess on the bottom turns, and I do mean a mess, I was still nineteenth. These had to be my race skis.

But seasons, like leopards, don't change their spots. For the umpteenth time, the race was postponed by bad weather. Again I had to unwind and then try to rekindle the zest and drive on another day.

When race day finally came, it was as though I had glue on the bottom of my skis. Only twenty yards out of the start I felt it was hardly worth going on. Just after the first interval time I made a small mistake that opened me up a little but I recovered to ski the bottom turns better than I had all week. But my final time on the clock was three seconds slower than my slowest practice time: a full six seconds behind the winner. It was agony. I was exhausted at the bottom, having fought to give my best: to see that time flash up on the board felt like a whiplash.

I sat for an hour and a half in the finish area stunned to silence and alone. I watched everyone come down – all faster than me bar three: I was fourth last.

Later I talked to Ernst Habbesatter, my mechanic, while we watched the race on video. He said: 'Of course you were slow, look at that jump.' He was referring to the small mistake I had made after the first interval time. That was typical of a mechanic, to blame the slowness on the racer. But it wasn't that easy. Certainly I wasn't skiing as well as I knew I should, but to be second fastest one day and three seconds behind the field the next on flats where it's well-nigh impossible to make a mistake was not on. It was a ski preparation fault – there was no other answer. Certainly Ernst was unable to come up with one when I put it to him like that.

That night I wasn't even able to drown my sorrows. We had to leave Aspen almost immediately by bus to get to Denver for the flight to the last race at Lake Louise. There is nothing more depressing after doing badly in a race than packing your bags, so I took some time off from this to see Steve Podborski, who had crashed and hurt himself in the race. In spite of that he had a smile on his face – not much of one, but compared with mine it was a grin. He asked me how I had done and I could still hardly believe it as I heard myself say I came fourth last. I can hardly believe it to this day.

The race had been won by Canadian Todd Brooker, who was on the same bus to Denver. Todd was excitedly loading up with beer for the journey; it was going to be a wild trip. But not for me. I was still shaking my head with disbelief and found myself talking to Swiss racer Toni Buergler, who was just as miserable as I was. Toni had had good practice runs all season and had been skiing well but had ended up, just like me, without results. It was somehow comforting to find a Swiss skier with the same problems as an English skier.

My second big surprise of the day came when Ken Read told me of his decision to retire after Lake Louise.

The accommodation at Lake Louise did nothing for my state of mind. It was more like the wartime days when my father had been there than a hotel. My room had a bunk bed and a couple of singles; I felt more like a schoolboy in a dormitory than a World Cup racer. It was there that I made my decision to retire. I rang my parents in Austria to tell them, and I rang Shauna in London but she replied: 'I already know.' It later transpired that John Samuel had scooped me. I had talked with him after the Aspen race and John had written my retirement piece from that, even though I hadn't made the final decision. I wasn't upset by this – rather I found it amusing, and it cost John a good dinner!

Once I had made my decision a weight was lifted from my shoulders, but I still wanted to do well in the last race; to go out in a blaze of glory, so to speak. But this wasn't to be. I liked the course and I thought I skied it well, but my time on the clock made me glad it was my last race.

After the race the Canadians made something of a fuss of me. I was interviewed for the papers and the team members all wished me well. They had good reason to, since I had just joined the army of unemployed. I told Koni and Ernst of my decision and I was interviewed by ITV (an interview that was never used).

I was glad I had retired in Canada. Their team had given me some of my best moments and some of my best friends. Now, on retirement, they treated me almost as one of their own. I felt that at least in Canada I was appreciated.

The night I had a wild dinner with Todd Brooker, Ken Read, Robin McLeish and their wives and girlfriends, and we washed away the agony with the ecstasy of a cocktail called 'B52'. I can't quite remember what was in it, but it had the desired effect: my flight out of skiing was on the wings of a cocktail named after a bomber!

A FINAL WORD

After so many years 'on the road', my life based on physical and mental experiences, the translation of them was a formidable task for Malcolm Severs. To package my thoughts and feelings into a legible collection of sentences and paragraphs required great commitment, enormous concentration and consummate skill. I would like to thank Malcolm for his patience and enthusiasm, and especially for his ability to extract every detail from my sometimes reluctant memory.

Although one stands alone on the skis, there have been many people whose support and encouragement has allowed me to attempt to achieve one of my goals. To the industry, the clubs, many friends in the press and television, and to the individuals who thought or hoped that it was possible, I would like to offer my full appreciation.

To my family, thank you.

KONRAD BARTELSKI